PHOTOGRAPHERS' BRITAIN

SOMERSET

PHOTOGRAPHERS' BRITAIN

SOMERSET

CHRIS WILLOUGHBY

ALAN SUTTON

First published in the United Kingdom in 1993
Alan Sutton Publishing · Phoenix Mill · Far Thrupp · Stroud · Gloucestershire

First published in the United States of America in 1993
Alan Sutton Publishing Inc · 83 Washington Street · Dover NH 03820

British Library Cataloguing in Publication Data

Willoughby, Chris
Photographers' Britain: Somerset
I. Title
779.994238

ISBN 0-7509-0105-5

Library of Congress Cataloging-in-Publication Data applied for

Cover photograph: Glastonbury Tor
Endpapers: front: Thorn tree, Exmoor; *back*: Winter flooding, Curry Moor
Title page photograph: Parrock Hill

Typeset in 10/14 Sabon.
Typesetting and origination by
Alan Sutton Publishing Limited.
Printed in Great Britain by
The Bath Press, Avon.

INTRODUCTION

In the spring of 1976 I left the industrial Midlands, where I had worked in a photographic studio specializing in advertising, for rural Somerset. It was quite by chance that I settled in Burrowbridge in the heart of the wetland region of the county, known as the Sedgemoor. I was immediately struck by the uniqueness of this landscape. For the next five years I spent every available moment exploring the region, photographing both the landscape and the people who lived there.

Here, some 3,000 years BC, the first settlers arrived. During the summer months the flood waters would recede from these lowlands, leaving behind them areas of pastureland, lakes and marshes rich in fish and wildlife. Villages were built on slightly higher ground, and their inhabitants were responsible for the construction of the oldest known road system, based on floating trackways. A number of examples have been discovered perfectly preserved in the peat moors near Glastonbury. Later, the Saxons who moved here became known as the 'Somerseaten' – those who lived by the lakes. Others have referred to Somerset as the land of the 'summer-settlers', hill people who, during the summer months, descended from the surrounding hills to graze their livestock on the rich pastureland of the Sedgemoor.

But there is more to the county than 100,000 hectares of wetland, for Somerset contains an extraordinary diverse range of topographical features, both natural and man-made. To the north, running almost east–west, are the bleak and windswept limestone hills of the Mendips. From a distance these hills appear featureless and uninteresting, but closer inspection reveals a landscape cleft by ravines, riddled by caves and underground rivers, and ravaged for centuries by the activities of miners and quarrymen. South-west of the Mendips and the wetlands are four more ranges of hills – the Quantocks, Brendons, Blackdowns and Exmoor, which straddles both Somerset and Devon, and is now a national park. Each area has its own particular qualities and history. Between these hilly ranges there are the gentler valleys of fields, villages and towns, including Wells, the smallest cathedral city in England. The northern boundary

PORLOCK HARBOUR

of the county is formed by the Bristol Channel. To the west the hills of Exmoor plunge into the sea; here the coastline is craggy and storm swept. It is here that the pent-up energy of the Atlantic is finally unleashed on to the shoreline. As one travels eastwards rocky cliffs give way gradually to more gentle, but no less interesting coastline. Around Kilve and East Quantoxhead the beaches are made up of slabs or pavements of limestone, that in places appear almost man-made. The eerie desolation of Hinkley Point marks the spot of both a petrified forest and one of Britain's first nuclear power stations. From there as far as Brean Down the coastline curves northwards and the landward side of the county dips away from the shore, the coast forming a protective lip, rather like that of a shallow saucer.

From a photographic standpoint the county of Somerset provides quite a challenge, for it has so much to offer. No matter that much of it has already been documented, for one of the positive aspects of the rapidly changing English weather ensures a constant variation of light and atmospheric conditions. Therefore no two ways will be precisely the same, providing the photographer with the opportunity to record what is genuinely a unique experience.

I would like to acknowledge the help of the following: the staff of the Somerset Local History Library, Taunton; Philip Stoyle of Bridgwater Library reference section; Peter Bartlett; and the Exmoor Pony Society.

BREAN DOWN

If you take Frome on the Wiltshire border as the eastern boundary of the Mendips, and from here travel slightly north of west, you will eventually reach their most westerly extremity at Brean Down.

Once an isolated outcrop of limestone rock surrounded by sea, Brean Down is now joined to the mainland by a narrow isthmus of reclaimed marshland. Its geographical position overlooking the Bristol Channel and the river Axe has made it an ideal position for fortifications since the Iron Age up until the Second World War. There is little evidence of the Iron Age fort or the Roman temple, which was built in AD 367 and lasted for over 130 years. It is now only a few slight undulations in the ground. But at the very western tip of the headland, with a clear 180 degree view southwards across Bridgwater Bay to the approaches of the river Severn in the north, is a disused gun battery and soldiers' quarters. The emplacement dates from the Napoleonic Wars and directly adjacent to this, below the cliffs, a short length of narrow gauge railway runs out towards the sea. At the very end of the line and out to one side there is a small rectangular flat roofed concrete building. This is all that remains of a Second World War special sound effects station. It was from here that sound signals, which were designed to disorientate German acoustic torpedoes and render them ineffective, were transmitted through the waters of the Bristol Channel.

Brean Down is now a nature reserve, its remote position and maritime environment providing the right conditions for a number of rare plants including the hair grass and the goldilocks flower. Brean Down and four other sites across the British Isles are the only places you will find this particular flower. Occasional sightings of ravens have been made here, but what you are most likely to see are the wild goats, especially the males with their long scimitar like horns, standing on some rocky ledge watching over the rest of the herd as they leap and bound effortlessly along the cliff sides above the sea.

DRYSTONE WALLS, MENDIP HILLS

The loneliness of the Mendips is a real loneliness. A man turns to the sky because he must; he is shut away from the great and fruitful world he knows, the towns, the villages and ploughfields beneath him, not only by the height but also by the breadth and flatness of the great plateau, which the roads, purposeless for the most part, shepherded by their loose walls of grey stone, traverse so swiftly, anxious only to pass on their endless ways. One is caught as it were in an empty space, a featureless desolation, a solitude like no other solitude.

So wrote Edward Hutton in 1912 in his *Highways and Byways of Somerset*. From 1750 to 1850 the Mendip hills came under the influence of the enclosure acts: land that was regarded as common was divided up into recognizable fields with definite boundaries. This meant the planting of hedges or fence building, both of which were expensive and labour intensive. The soil of the Mendips is thin and the hills were, in the pre-industrial age, sparsely populated, so the cost of producing traditional field boundaries would have been too high. The limestone rock which makes up much of the Mendips appears very close to the surface, and also splits naturally into roughly rectangular shapes. So by clearing the land of large stones to make it suitable for sowing, a ready made source of building material became available. These walls were relatively cheap to build, requiring no mortar in their construction, and could easily be altered or even knocked down so that the materials could be reused – to build farm buildings, to be burned for lime production or for the construction of roads. The walls too provided a certain amount of protection against the cold winds for both livestock and wildlife. It is a favoured home for England's only venomous snake, the adder, and a particularly unusual variety of black adder that lives around the village of Priddy.

CHARTERHOUSE RAKES

The Mendips, which run almost east–west along the northern borders of Somerset, appear from a distance a smooth surfaced, rounded and relatively featureless range of hills. Their apparent softness of outline, especially during the early morning or late afternoon, belies a harshness that has to be experienced to be believed.

At one of the highest points and certainly one of the bleakest lie the remains of the Charterhouse Lead Mines. These limestone hills were once rich in minerals such as lead and silver ores. The Romans were the first to exploit these resources and left ample evidence of their excavations. The rounded hillsides around Charterhouse are scarred with rocky ravines and curious undulating humps of slag now covered in tussocky grass, rather like the inside surface of an eggbox, but on a vast scale. Limestone is a porous rock that allows any rain water to percolate rapidly through the surface and form underground rivers, tunnels and caves. Later generations of lead miners were to use these tunnels.

All the workable lead deposits have long gone, and the mines are abandoned. The tunnels and caves and underground rivers attract new sorts of adventurer, the potholer and the cave diver. It is not an uncommon sight to see, as one clambers around this craggy landscape, the occasional helmeted figure, face black with grime, emerge grinning from the top of one of these tussocky hummocks.

Sun Street, Frome

The wealth of Frome was built on the woollen industry, the nearby chalk uplands of Wiltshire providing the ideal pasture for sheep grazing. There are many fine buildings in Frome that reflect the town's one time prosperity, but one area of the town is often overlooked. Frome contains one of the oldest examples of purpose-built housing for industrial workers. The area of Frome known as the Trinity district contains many simple but well-constructed houses, their distinctive features including some fine exterior and interior detailing.

The town never really recovered after the decline of the woollen industry. Over the years the Trinity district suffered neglect, through inadequate housing policies by both national and local governments. By the 1970s many of the houses lay derelict, their interiors plundered for the pine mouldings and fittings, and the area was considered by many to be a slum. By this time most of the inhabitants had been relocated to new housing nearby. However, in 1976 a firm of architects was commissioned to decide whether or not the houses were worth restoring. Fortunately the results of the study were favourable, stating that the houses were well designed and built and if repaired, would provide good quality housing for years to come.

The process of refurbishment still continues, and many of the houses have been restored with great care and sensitivity. Sun Street lies just outside the Trinity district, but is typical of the housing style to be found in Trinity itself.

SELWOOD PRINT WORKS, FROME

As mentioned before, the wealth of Frome was founded on the woollen industry, which is thought to have started as early as 1320. Frome enjoyed an enviable position as one of the country's foremost producers of woven material for nearly four hundred years. But it was an overriding conservatism within the industry that eventually led to its decline. Mechanization in the form of steam power was being introduced to the great textile mills of the north, Frome's traditional rivals, but the hand-weavers of Frome refused to move with the times, to their cost.

While the cloth industry slid into decline, new enterprises sprang up to take its place. One such business was the result of a part-time interest by a local chemist, a Mr Crocker, who chose to print his own labels. On his retirement the pharmacy was taken over by W. Langford, who continued with the printing sideline, but still on a small scale. In 1830 Mr Langford was joined by another chemist, W.T. Butler, to run the pharmacy as a partnership. It was during this time that the printing aspect of the business began to flourish, and by 1864 it had expanded to such an extent that Butler finally gave up his partnership as a chemist and set up the W.T. Butler Steam Printing Works. Frome was benefiting from the new rail links with other parts of the country, and cheap coal was available in nearby Radstock. The lesson learned from the fate of Frome's textile industry was a salutary one.

Shortly after the works settled into its new premises, a dynamic young man arrived on the scene. Mr Tanner, who had spent some time in the wool trade, encouraged W. Butler to invest heavily in the latest printing technology and to hire only the finest craftsmen. The relationship only lasted two years, but by this time the investment had paid off. The works then became known as Butler and Tanner Printers and still is to this day, while the new premises were called the Selwood Print Works after the forest that once surrounded the town. By 1884 Butler and Tanner were regarded as one of the country's foremost printers and had outgrown their Selwood plant.

Butler and Tanner continued to thrive at their new site close to the railway station, but the area of Trinity, where the Selwood works were situated, suffered a long period of neglect. Since then the building has been used for a number of business schemes including small workshop units and warehousing, but none of these has provided a long term solution for this building. Frome, like other parts of the country, is in the grip of a recession, and the Selwood building lies empty, its future undecided.

MOON'S HILL QUARRY

The Mendips have been exploited for their mineral resources for centuries. Making the most impression on the surrounding countryside have been the stone quarries, which can be found along the entire length of these hills. The stone for both Glastonbury Abbey and Wells Cathedral was taken from quarries in the Mendips.

The demand for stone for building purposes increased at a moderate rate until the Industrial Revolution. Industrialized towns need lines of communication, such as roads and railways, to survive, and the carboniferous limestone rock from the Mendips produces the ideal material for road building. With the railways declining in popularity in the 1950s so the expansion of road building began. Motorways demand vast quantities of material for their construction, and much of this comes from the quarries of the Mendip hills.

Moon's Hill quarry is situated at the eastern end of the Mendips. One approaches by way of narrow country lanes, and enters the quarry through a narrow gorge carved out of the hillside. There before you lies this crater, in fact a hill with its centre removed.

Emborough Pool

The Mendip hills are littered with caves, burial mounds and ravines. Some of these are natural occurrences, while others are the results of man's activities over the centuries. Emborough Pool is probably a natural phenomenon, a small lake of approximately 1½ hectares in size, surrounded on three sides by mature woodland.

The whole of the upper Mendip plateau could be described as having a certain desolate beauty. The lake is now a favourite spot for anglers and there are many who enjoy the peace of the woodland that surrounds the pool. But it has not always been so: a hundred years ago it was described as 'dismal sheet of water, a bottomless pit'. It seems that the pool was the scene of an unsolved tragedy. It is the story of a love affair between the son of a wealthy mine owner and a maid, who worked at a manor house nearby. The girl became pregnant and, when discovered, incurred the wrath of her father and was banned from seeing the boy again. The boy was ostracized by his family because of the scandal, and left home in despair. When he did not return a search party was sent out from the village, and during the search articles of clothing were found floating in Emborough Pool. His mother confirmed that they were her son's, and of course she feared the worst. But despite dragging the pond twice no trace of a body was ever found.

BRENT KNOLL

Just south of the Mendips the landscape is dominated by a series of conically shaped hills. These were at one time islands, the most famous being Glastonbury Tor. Although there are several historical and legendary connections with the Tor, Brent Knoll has been largely overlooked as a landmark. No recent scientific studies have been made of the hill-fort that forms the crown of the hill, since the work done by the Revd Mr Skinner during the early part of the nineteenth century. From his casual excavations of the centre of the fort it would seem that the Romans established fortified position here, making use of an existing Iron Age settlement.

The disentanglement of fact from fiction is not always a straightforward task, for in medieval times monks embellished their accounts with liberal quantities of myth. The Glastonbury monks were no exception, for they were anxious to establish the pedigree of their monastery. It was done by skilfully blending the legends of King Arthur with facts about their own history. William of Malmesbury, a chronicler of the monastic life of Glastonbury Abbey during the early part of the twelfth century, records how Ider, son of one of King Arthur's knights, a King Nuth, fought and killed three giants on the Mount of Frogs, now referred to as Brent Knoll. Alfred, believing Ider to have lost his life during the fight, felt responsible, and in order to do penance presented the abbey with lands surrounding Brent Knoll. During the reign of Ine (688–726), the king of the West Saxons, large parcels of land around the Knoll were presented to Abbot Hemgisl for use by the abbey. Brent Knoll was held by Glastonbury until the Dissolution of the Monasteries in 1536.

It is possible that the hill provided a landmark for ships travelling up the Bristol Channel. Before the building of the Trinity House lighthouses in Burnham-on-Sea in 1832, the church spire of East Brent was painted white as a navigational aid.

For a brief time during the Second World War the hill-fort reverted to its former role, when slit trenches and gun emplacements were dug into the ramparts as part of a Home Guard exercise in coastal defence. The hill looks most impressive from the M5 motorway, but this is not the best position from which to photograph it! Driving around the narrow lanes that skirt the base of Brent Knoll, I chanced upon this orchard. As I approached the line of apple trees, fighting buck rabbits scattered in all directions. The late afternoon sunlight provided the perfect conditions, and my first photograph provided the image I required.

EDITHMEAD CHURCH

Sometimes referred to affectionately as the Edithmead cathedral, this little church arrived here on the back of a horse and cart in about 1920. Quite a number of these corrugated iron churches can be found dotted around the peat moors or heaths surrounding Glastonbury, but most of them have been converted to either storerooms or workshops. During the latter part of the nineteenth century considerable improvements were made in iron foundry production, and it was during this time that iron began to be used as a building material. Mass production techniques enabled the production of low cost and durable metal buildings, which could be assembled on site. There were many firms at that time who specialized in new and second-hand churches, some of which were quite substantial – displaying highly ornate interiors made from cast iron, while others were plain and simple like that of Edithmead. Such buildings would have found favour with the inhabitants of the Somerset peat moors, partly because of their cost, for it is only recently that the commercial exploitation of peat has had any real impact on the area, and secondly because they would not have required a substantial base on which to be built. There is of course no significant bedrock here to provide really stable footings; evidence of subsidence is everywhere. Another advantage of this particular method of construction, judging by the evidence of a second-hand trade, was their portability. Here at Edithmead the building has been beautifully maintained, its paintwork fresh in a modest grey and white which blends perfectly with its surroundings, and what is more the church is still in regular use. A few days before this photograph was taken a wedding ceremony had been conducted here, together with a congregation of well over forty guests.

THE WOODEN LIGHTHOUSE

Built by Trinity House to guide shipping up the treacherous waters of the River Parrett, this wooden lighthouse looks like a child's impression of a primitive robot gazing out to sea. It is no longer used as a lighthouse, having been replaced by a more traditionally built one further onshore, and now acts as a leading mark for the few ships that enter the channel to make their way upstream to the port of Dunball. At low water you can still see the carcass of the wrecked sailing ship, the *Nornen*, that was blown ashore during a gale in 1887. Shipwrecks are few and far between now – only the occasional grounding by yachts unfamiliar with local conditions perhaps – thanks to modern navigational aids and an efficient pilot service.

However, if you stroll along the water's edge at low tide, you may just come across the odd car roof poking through the surface of the fine sand – a victim of the tides. The Bristol Channel experiences the second highest tidal range in the world. It is all too tempting to drive your car on to the beach and go off for a walk, but when the tide turns it comes in at an alarming rate.

SEA WALL, BURNHAM-ON-SEA

The Somerset levels are a narrow strip of coastland lying at or slightly below the high tide mark, stretching from just west of Bridgwater to Brean Down on the Avon border. The land behind, the moors and heaths of Sedgemoor, in fact sink further down, forming a shallow basin of approximately 104,000 hectares. The importance of an effective sea defence system is paramount.

The tidal range in the Bristol Channel and the Severn Estuary is, as mentioned above, one of the highest in the world. During the winter months the prevailing south-westerly winds combine with the action of the tide to produce a considerable mass of water which surges up the narrow confines of the Bristol Channel. This action has been likened to a child sliding up and down in a bath full of water. On each consecutive slide the wall of water builds up further until eventually half the bath's contents spill over on to the bathroom floor. This is in effect what happened during a great storm in December 1981, one of the worst this century, although in this case it took more than a mop to clean up the mess. The force of the water constantly beating against the old sea wall gradually undermined its foundations, and during the night there were terrific explosions as the full might of the storm waters burst through the surface of the road that lay alongside the wall. As dawn broke a scene of utter devastation was revealed and a row of craters could be seen all along the sea front of the town. The damage was not confined to this area alone; further west, the sea had broken through and had rushed in causing severe flooding several miles inland.

The damage was so serious all along this stretch of coast that a major construction project was undertaken, costing £7 million and taking five years to complete. The result is the highest wave return wall in Britain, standing some 3.2 metres above the beach. The graceful curve of the wall, itself like a frozen wave, rolls the powerful storm waves back the way they came, the steps below absorbing their energy.

BRIDGWATER BAY

The long sweeping curve of Bridgwater Bay stretches from Hinkley Point in the southwest to Brean Down in the north. The coastline along this part of Somerset is rather like the lip of a shallow bowl. The lip itself is in places only a few metres above the sea while the land behind falls away, the bottom of the bowl being several kilometres inland. It is a bay that is swept with vicious currents, and contains no sheltered inlets, picturesque fishing harbours or sophisticated holiday resorts, only miles of mud and a frothy brown sea that laps on its shore. For the more ambitious explorer this coastline has much to offer. Adjacent to the nuclear power station at Hinkley Point, with its own inherent mysteries, is a nature reserve. The nutrient-rich mudflats exposed at low water provide the ideal feeding grounds for many species of sea bird. Along the pebble beach you can find many fossilized remains of ammonites, some weighing between 10 and 15 kilograms each.

One boundary of the reserve is Stert Point at the mouth of the River Parrett. If you were to travel up this river you might catch a glimpse of a salmon, struggling to the surface for air. The water is so laden with silt here that fish have to surface to clear their gills of mud. Local fishermen have exploited this and employ a technique known as salmon dipping. This involves chasing the salmon from a small boat and estimating where the unfortunate fish will surface. A net fixed to a long pole is lowered into the water, and the salmon is scooped out – if the fisherman judges right.

From the River Parrett the coastline travels due north, taking in the resorts of Burnham-on-Sea and Brean Sands, a huge expanse of hard flat sand bordered by dunes to the east.

The bay ends abruptly with Brean Down, below the cliffs of which a spectacular civil engineering project has been proposed. The intention is to build a tidal barrage from this point on the Somerset coast across the Bristol Channel to the South Wales coast, a total of 16 kilometres. The barrage would contain lock gates to allow the passage of shipping, a dual carriageway road system linking the West Country with South Wales, but more importantly still a series of turbines that would convert the tremendous power of the tides into electricity. The power generated by this means would provide anything up to 7 per cent of the nation's needs. As with all such schemes there is a price to pay, not only financially. Conservationists have argued that the Severn Estuary and the shoreline of the Bristol Channel provides one of the most important feeding grounds for migrating birds in the northern hemisphere, and that the construction of this barrage would destroy it for ever.

CHEDDAR GORGE

This is certainly the most spectacular sight to be seen in Somerset. The gorge cuts deeply into the Mendip Hills, the sheer sides rising vertically to a height of 130 metres in places. The gorge was formed during the last Ice Age: the melt water from glaciers further north produced fast-flowing streams that cut through the porous limestone of the Mendips.

A guide to Somerset written in 1912 gives this advice to visitors to the gorge:

The wise traveller will always approach Cheddar from the hills, thus descending the gorge, and this is for two reasons. In the first place the mere effect is infinitely more astonishing, for the spectacle increases in splendour and height as he descends. In the second place the rabble of touts, the confusion of bustling advertisements, and the air of Bank Holiday that overwhelms the town of Cheddar at the foot of the gorge are enough to spoil most people's enjoyment of nature. If one descends from the silence of the great plateau, one comes to all this noise when the great spectacle has passed, and one can pass through it without delay.

This may still be true today, but it is interesting to note that before the opening of the gorge and its caves to tourists in 1908, many people in this area of Somerset derived their living from lead mining. Conditions were appalling and the ore was running out. The miners themselves and often their families lived in the numerous caves to be found along the gorge. Who can blame them for seeking an alternative source of income? Anything would have been preferable to this horrendous underground existence.

The gorge runs approximately north-east to south-west, and at certain times of the year the setting sun shines directly along the length of the canyon, casting long cool shadows along the valley floor. Without the sun's warmth the crowds soon disappear. A brisk climb brings you to the plateau above the gorge, and with it silence and the stunning views in both directions. To the west lies Brent Knoll, the Bristol Channel and the setting sun, and to the east the whole spectacle of the gorge itself.

WELLS CATHEDRAL – THE WEST FRONT

At the centre of the smallest city in England stands one of the most beautiful cathedrals in Europe. For twelve centuries there has been a church at Wells, the first being a shrine constructed by the Saxon king Ine. Much of what we see today dates from the twelfth century. The cathedral is spectacular from all directions, but nothing quite compares with the west front. This represents the final stage in the work that began in 1180. It was Bishop Jocelyn, appointed as Bishop of Wells in 1207, who instigated the building of this façade. The original part of the cathedral was worked in the traditional West Country style, but by the time the work on the west front had begun, new craftsmen had been employed. Adam Lock and Thomas Norreys were more cosmopolitan men, the great cathedrals of France and northern Spain providing their inspiration. The west front took a long time to complete, almost two hundred years including the two towers. The intention was to create a spectacular display of religious sculptures, and the façade is today regarded as one of the finest examples of Gothic sculpture in the world. Originally the central part would have been painted, the statues decorated in gold, red, blues and ochres standing out against a backdrop of whitewashed masonry. The subsequent years have taken their toll, many statues being damaged by drunken vandals during the latter part of the seventeenth century. In more recent times atmospheric pollution has been the principal cause of the façade's decay. Sulphur dioxide in the air combines with compounds in the limestone to form crystalline salts of magnesium and calcium sulphate. As the crystals accumulate within the statue, the structure of the stone becomes brittle and begins to disintegrate. Reversing this process appears to be more difficult to achieve. In 1977 a scheme began to clean, restore and conserve all the sculptures on the west front. Ten years later this was completed; several new conservation techniques were used and only time will tell whether they prove to be successful. The façade now enjoys a new lease of life which cannot fail to impress even the most jaded of visitors.

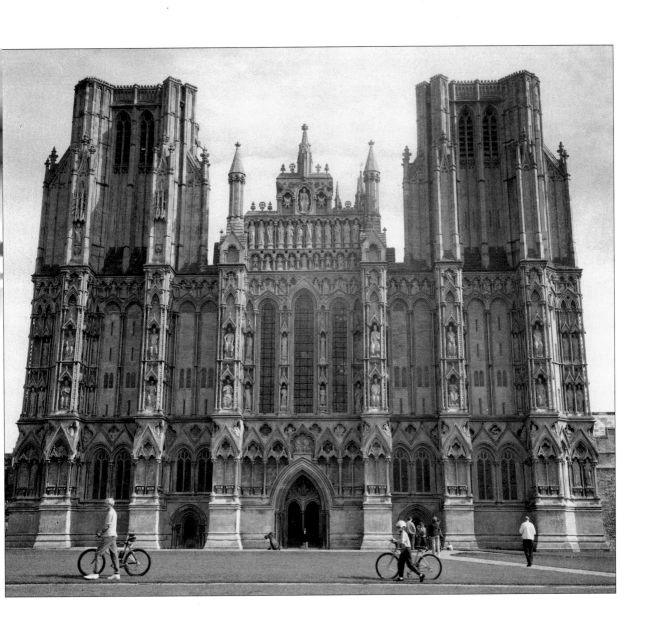

BRIDGWATER FLATNER

It was the name Black Rock that first attracted me to this desolate spot at the mouth of the River Parrett. It is a flat treeless landscape with only the river bank offering any shelter from the chill wind that blows off the Bristol Channel to the North.

The tide here ebbs and flows at a ferocious rate. At every low tide thousands of tons of thick brown ooze are deposited on to these banks. This small rocky outcrop provides the base for Bob Thornes' salmon fishing enterprise. Wooden fishtraps called 'butts' are staked out into the river facing upstream, trapping the fish as they struggle against the outgoing tide. To service these butts at high water Bob Thorne makes use of a flat-bottomed boat known as the Bridgwater flatner. Like the salmon butts the flatner has evolved over a long period of time. It is thought to be the direct descendant of the dugout canoe. At one time the banks of the Parrett were lined with these seaworthy craft, their flat–bottomed shape enabling them to slide over the mudflats into deeper water. Their symmetry and pureness of line demonstrates a rare quality that combines both craft and function in a perfect marriage. This particular boat was built by John Carter in 1947 using only locally found materials, elm planking on oak frames, for the princely sum of £1 17s 6d, including sails.

WESTHAY DISUSED PEAT WORKINGS

The extraction of peat from the ground leaves large areas of hollowed out land, which invariably fill up with water. There have been suggestions that these sites should be turned over to leisure pursuits, such as boating and water skiing; fortunately, more enlightened landowners have allowed their workings to revert to a wild state. Just a few metres from the road you can plunge into head-high grasses and catch glimpses of wild deer, leaping and bounding off into denser undergrowth. It is easy to imagine yourself deep in the central African plains. These tiny sanctuaries provide essential breeding grounds for our wildlife. The formation of the peat moors resulted in the depletion of calcium salts and an increase in the acidity of the soil. Consequently only plants that could survive these conditions flourished. Some of the more unusual plants include the insectivorous varieties such as the bladderwort and the bog bean, which derive their nutrients from the insects they ensnare in their leaves. The high water table encourages an abundance of insect and rodent species, which in turn provide food for predatory birds. The harrier is now classified as a rare bird nationally, in particular the marsh harrier, which breeds in small numbers on the peat moors. This is why on my second visit to this location I found my way barred by a very efficient looking warden fully equipped with binoculars and portable phone. My name was taken and I was told that on no account could I proceed any further into the reserve – a great disappointment. On reflection, however, I realized that this is regrettably the only way to preserve what is left of our rural heritage.

PEAT STACKS

The melting of the polar ice caps approximately eight thousand years ago caused the sea level to rise, flooding the valleys between the Mendip and Quantock hills. This marine flooding allowed large deposits of clay and alluvial silt to settle on the valley floor. As the sea level dropped slightly the exposed mudflats were able to support plants such as the reed. During the winter months the leaves of the plant would die and form a layer of rotting vegetation, in turn providing a base for further plant species including the sedge. The continuous cycle of growth and decay gradually built up a layer of densely compacted vegetation. Climatic changes around 3,000 BC produced a new variety of plant life that could cope with the increased rainfall, such a plant being the sphagnum moss, which is the main constituent of the peat formed during this period. The continuing heavy rainfall began to alter the soil conditions drastically, leaching out the rich calcium salts and producing an acid peat, which carried on growing in depth until AD 300. It is this layer of peat that is now visible at the surface of the moors around Glastonbury.

As in Ireland the peat was originally dug purely for burning. The peat moors were regarded as common land, where the locals had free access to extract the peat for their own use. This was done until recently by hand. First the vegetation and topsoil were removed to expose a strip of peat approximately 4 metres wide. An incision was made in the peat with the blade of a hay knife, and rectangular blocks or mumps were dug out with a spade and placed on one side to dry. Digging peat by hand is back breaking work, and often takes place in damp conditions. In 1870, when commercial extraction began, peat diggers' wages were supplemented with copious quantities of cider.

Today the peat is cut by machine, which lays the mumps in rows to dry, in much the same way as before. Once the blocks are part dry they are rearranged into conically shaped mounds or ruckles for further drying, the whole process taking about a year. The peat is then removed to the packing sheds where it is ground into granules and bagged, ready to be shipped off to garden centres around the country. Over 90 per cent of all peat extracted is now sold for horticultural purposes.

GLASTONBURY TOR

England's Fujiyama seems to me to be one of the best descriptions of Glastonbury Tor. This conical hill which rises out of the surrounding wetlands has been a potent mystical symbol for a succession of pilgrims of various religious persuasions over the centuries. The whole of the Glastonbury region is immersed in a tangled web of history and legend and the Tor itself provides a natural focal point. The Christian legend states that Joseph of Arimathea set sail for England some years after the death of Christ, accompanied by a few friends, and eventually ended up at the base of the Tor. Joseph apparently believed that the Tor closely resembled the Mount of Transfiguration and decided to establish a Christian community here, building what many people regard to be the first Christian church in England, a simple affair constructed of wattle and daub. At the base of the Tor lies the Chalice Well where it is believed that Joseph buried the chalice from the Last Supper. Many claim that the spring that emanates from this spot contains a healing property, a belief that probably predates Christianity. There has been no hard scientific evidence yet to verify this legend. Apart from a few scattered Roman remains found around the vicinity of the Tor, the earliest evidence of a community dates from the sixth century AD. It seems that the occupiers of this community built some sort of timber structure on the summit of the hill, engaged in metalworking and, judging by the quantity of animal bones left behind, were great consumers of meat. All this points to a fortified position rather than a place of worship, and some would say that this would tie in with the Arthurian legends that are also closely associated with Glastonbury. In the late Saxon and early medieval times a small monastic order was established here, and it was this that built the first stone church, dedicated to St Michael. Today the current vogue for alternative beliefs provides a steady flow of visitors, who see the Tor as a symbol of pre-Christian energies and, judging by the number of publications to be had in local bookshops, theories of ley lines and earth goddesses abound. Perhaps one day we will discover the true story or stories behind Glastonbury Tor, but in the meantime this distinctive landmark will provide the focus for many a pilgrim whether Christian, pagan or just plain curious.

GLASTONBURY ABBEY

Lying as it does at the base of the Tor, the history of the abbey is very much enmeshed with that of the Tor. The mysteries surrounding the origins of this monument will undoubtedly continue for many years to come. Legend and fact are once again inextricably linked. The story of Jesus as a young boy travelling to the West Country with his uncle, Joseph of Arimathea, a tin trader, to buy Cornish tin and Mendip lead, is said to have inspired William Blake's hymn 'And did those feet in ancient times walk upon England's pastures green'. The story goes on to state that Joseph, some thirty years after Jesus's death, returned to Glastonbury to found the first Christian church. Research has revealed that those stories are medieval in origin dating from a period in which the abbey at Glastonbury was keen to establish itself within the hierarchy of the church establishment. History tells us it was the great Saxon king Ine who established Glastonbury as a religious centre, and the Abbot Dunstan who founded a Benedictine order here during the twelfth century. Dunstan was a learned man of many talents, both as an artist and musician, who rose in eminence to become the Archbishop of Canterbury.

In 1184 a great fire destroyed the wooden church and the many buildings that surrounded it, but the monks, some would say fortuitously, claimed to have discovered the remains of King Arthur and Guinevere. This resurrected the cult of Arthur as a popular hero, ensuring a steady flow of pilgrims who were willing to subscribe to the rebuilding of the abbey. This rebuilding formed the basis of what we see today. The enlargement of the abbey continued steadily after King Henry II's death in 1189, for at least another three hundred years, ending with the last of the great builders, Abbot Bere, who died in 1524. Bere was succeeded by Abbot Whyting, a highly educated man who was noted for his generosity to the poor. Sadly he fell prey to King Henry VIII and in 1538, when he refused to submit to the king's demands for the disbanding of the abbey, was arrested on a trumped up charge for treason. Despite his frailty and age, for he was ninety years old by this time, he was tried and condemned to death. From his place of trial he was dragged to the top of the Tor and hanged, drawn and quartered. The abbey, once in the king's possession was abandoned, and the buildings plundered for their stone, to be used for houses and roads. It is claimed that the Abbey was so well constructed that gunpowder had to be used to dislodge the masonry. It was also reported at the time that buildings made from the abbey's remains did not last long and would fall down mysteriously, a suggestion perhaps of divine revenge.

BUTLEIGH COURT

Originally a long low simple house, Butleigh Court was transformed into a grand building, incorporating a hotchpotch of architectural styles, by the Grenville family. In order to complete this transformation the Grenvilles insisted on taking some consecrated ground belonging to the church next door. This infuriated some of Butleigh's inhabitants, as it meant that graves had to be moved. The aggrieved locals took their revenge by placing a curse on the Grenville family, or so the story goes. Certainly the last of the family line, Neville Grenville, died (in 1936) without an heir and the house and estate were abandoned, falling into dereliction.

Despite the curse Neville Grenville lived the life of a gentleman inventor, for he was a man of considerable technological flair and craftsmanship. In his own workshops he built steam lorries and traction engines, which he put to good use around his farm. The house also has a number of interesting features, one being a complex system of ducts built into the walls, that channelled air around the house, thus keeping it warm and dry.

The house itself is set in magnificent grounds, containing many unusual trees, including avenues of cedars, one of the first sequoia trees outside Kew, and many fine English oaks. After trying many viewpoints, in an attempt to capture the quintessential English scene – sheep grazing among the oak trees in front of the stately home – I settled for a straightforward shot of the front elevation. After all, it was the exotic nature of this façade that first attracted my attention.

CADBURY CASTLE – CAMELOT

Archaeological research has provided evidence that Cadbury Castle was used as a fortified position from 3,000 BC. Its importance as a castle continued until the eleventh century.

In AD 70 the Romans made their stronghold here, and in AD 500 further developments took place including the building of massive fortifications. A prosperous and highly organized society of military people lived here. In 1542 the historian Leland first refers to the Camelot of Arthurian legend. There are three possible sites for Camelot in the West Country, but it would seem that if Arthur reigned at all he would have based himself here. From the summit of the castle you have a commanding view of the surrounding country on all sides. The central part of the castle area is open and slightly domed in shape; the upper ramparts, which are very steep sided, are open too. There is, however, no evidence left of any building work here at all, although marked on the Ordnance Survey are two wells, King Arthur's and St Anne's, one on each side of the fortification.

To enter the castle you must first climb the path that takes you through the heavily wooded lower ramparts, the branches of the mature oaks and beech trees forming a tunnel to the summit. Once there, you can only be impressed by the sheer size of the fort. To convey all of this in one photograph was a difficult task, but the dying hawthorn tree provided a suitable device to help frame the composition.

BRIDGWATER CLAY PITS

The rich deposits of alluvial clay to be found along the River Parrett valley were the obvious reason for the flourishing brick and tile industry in the late eighteenth century. At one time over 250 firms were employed making clay products, including the famous Bridgwater Double Roman roof tile. The clay was easily extracted from pits around Bridgwater, together with the slime, a clay deposit left by the outgoing tide from the River Parrett. Mass-production techniques and an increase in the use of cement-based products finally finished off the industry. The pits have been abandoned now and have been left to revert to a wild state, providing the perfect haven for flora and fauna.

Making my way through the tall reeds, listening to the distant call of a heron, it was difficult to believe that the M5 motorway lay less than a kilometre away, and immediately behind that the town of Bridgwater. A narrow gap in a wall of reeds provided the opportunity to combine all the pictorial elements, a glimpse of the still dark waters through the vertical lines of the reeds contrasting with avenues of soft cumulus clouds in the sky.

FROM KING'S SQUARE TO CASTLE STREET

From 1645 Charles I, believing Bridgwater to be surrounded by impregnable marshes, placed great store by the security of his castle at Bridgwater. Despite being manned by a force of over 1,000 officers and men, equipped with at least forty cannon, it fell after a brief attack by the Parliamentary forces under General Fairfax. Some forty years later the castle played host to the ill-fated Duke of Monmouth, who rode out to his final defeat at the Battle of Sedgemoor. From then on the castle gradually fell into a state of disrepair.

In 1721 a wealthy businessman, the Duke of Chandos, bought the castle with an eye for redevelopment. The Duke had already invested large amounts of his own money into local enterprises, hoping to transform Bridgwater into a centre for commerce and industry. Ropemaking, shipbuilding, soap manufacturing and a glass works were some of his projects. It was his opinion that those who were to manage these businesses would require well–appointed accommodation, and so it was here within the castle precincts that the duke decided to build a street of prestigious properties. Despite a distinctive lack of financial success with his industrial enterprises it has been estimated that of the £15,000 the duke invested in Bridgwater over fourteen years, only £6,000 was recouped as income, the duke persevered with his house construction programme and commissioned the architect Benjamin Holloway to design and supervise the building of Castle Street. The stone from the derelict castle was salvaged and was either crushed to produce mortar or reused as a foundation material. The bricks for Castle Street were made by a local firm from Somerset clay. The houses continued in private ownership until 1902, when one side of the street was converted into the Mary Stanley nurses' training home. This institution, founded in memory of Queen Victoria, provided a nursing service to poor patients within their own homes free of charge. It eventually became a maternity hospital, which finally closed in 1985. On the opposite of the street is England's oldest regional arts centre, providing a venue for both the visual and performing arts.

Without a doubt a street of fine houses such as these looks better without rows of parked cars, often an impossible task. To get round this visual dilemma, a viewpoint from the neighbouring King's Square was selected, thus allowing a slight rise in the road surface to mask the offending vehicles.

The Castle House, Bridgwater

The Castle House is a unique nineteenth-century building, possibly the earliest example of precast concrete construction in the world. It takes its name from Bridgwater Castle, which was pulled down during the early part of the eighteenth century to make way for residential development. The Akerman family, who were local landowners and shareholders in Broad and Company, producers of lime and cement, commissioned the building of the Castle House in 1851. The architect who designed the building drew up plans as if it was to be made from stone, to demonstrate the fact that anything made from stone could be produced just as well from concrete. The house was to be a showcase to demonstrate the versatility of this material. The outside shell was made up from many precast concrete elements, including decorative panels, the modern versions of which can be found in builders' merchants and garden centres across the country and used as screens around many a suburban patio. Inside, cement and concrete were used on every possible occasion, as staircases, banisters and skirting boards. A number of innovative building techniques were tried out during the erection of the Castle House, including the first known use of constructional post tensioning. This is a method by which wires are passed through precast concrete so that it can withstand greater loadings than unstrengthed concrete. The wires are brought under tension either before the concrete has set, or, as in this case, at some period after setting is complete.

Despite attracting a lot of attention from conservationists, architects and building engineers, who see the building as a rare example of its kind, finances are not yet forthcoming to ensure the building's future. The house is now in a poor state, having recently been damaged by fire, and lies abandoned in the centre of Bridgwater.

The Taunton to Bridgwater Canal

Bridgwater is linked to the county town of Taunton by 22 kilometres of waterway. Officially opened in 1807, within two years of opening it was carrying well over 60,000 tonnes of cargo a year by horse-drawn barge. Originally the canal joined the River Parrett just upstream of Bridgwater, but in 1841 the canal was extended to the docks within Bridgwater itself and trade increased to a peak of 104,000 tonnes of cargo per year.

It was hoped that this stretch of canal would eventually link up with a much larger network of south-western waterways, which if completed would have joined Bridgwater and the Bristol Channel with Exeter and the shipping routes of the English Channel in the south. As with many other canals throughout the country, though, competition from the railways forced the Taunton and Bridgwater Canal into decline, and the last commercially operating barge ceased trading at the end of 1907.

Recent interest in the use of waterways as a leisure resource has saved the canal from total dereliction. The canal and lock system are now in full working order, providing a welcome escape for those who like to drift sedately through the Somerset countryside.

THE TEMPLE OF HARMONY

The Temple of Harmony was designed and built by Thomas Prowse in 1764, after the Temple of Fortuna Virilis in Rome dating from 1 BC. It was one of many follies that graced the Halswell House estate, some 60 hectares of landscaped gardens. The house was built for the Halswell family in 1536, and in 1650 the last of the line of Halswells, Jane, married a John Tynte. In 1674 the house was left to John's son, who later became Sir Halswell Tynte, and it was Sir Halswell's youngest son, Charles, who decided to devote over forty years of his life to the creation of a 'Somerset Arcadia'. Sir Charles Halswell Tynte was a personal friend of the Hoares, the banking family who created the famous house and gardens at Stourhead in Wiltshire, and although not as wealthy, Sir Charles endeavoured to produce a garden of comparable splendour. Like Stourhead, the gardens at Halswell made great use of water. At one time there were eight follies dotted around the estate and each was designed to evoke a differing emotion. To gain the full benefit of the overall design, a visitor to the gardens would have been conducted around a predetermined route. Having passed sinister looking grottos in dark and dank woodlands, the visitor would eventually find himself in open countryside, and there before him, surrounded by lakes and open pasture, would be the Temple of Harmony. The tranquillity of the scene ensured a sense of well-being and pleasure.

Shortly after the Second World War the house and garden were sold to a local entrepreneur, who sold off much of the land and converted the house into flats. Since then the house has been largely neglected, and both the garden and the follies have been allowed to fall into disrepair. Fortunately all is not lost, for two enthusiasts, John Tuckey and Timothy Davey, have bought the property and, undaunted by the enormity of the task, are devoting their energies to the complete restoration of what some regard to be the greatest undiscovered landscape gardens in England today.

Battle of Sedgemoor

A short walk along one of the droves near Westonzoyland, one comes to a rather forlorn and melancholy monument, which marks the site of the last battle to be fought on English soil.

It was on the night of 5 July 1685 that the rebel army led by the Duke of Monmouth set out from Bridgwater Castle to do battle with the king. It had been noted by an officer of the Royal Horse Guards that although it was nearly midsummer and a full moon was shining, 'the marsh fog lay so thick on Sedgemoor that no object could be discerned there at the distance of fifty paces'.

Any optimism felt by the rebel army as they left the confines of the castle, buoyed up by the cheering crowds, dwindled as open countryside beckoned. There was no beating of drums, no morale boosting songs, only the silence of the moors and the all engulfing mist. Around 1 a.m. they found themselves in open moorland, knowing full well that somewhere in the mists lay the enemy. The fields were surrounded by ditches or rhynes, some a mere 2 metres wide, others much wider and deeper. To begin with, all went well for the rebel army as they negotiated the narrow bridges that cross the rhynes until they reached the Langmoor rhyne. Unable to find the crossing point, they hesitated and in the confusion, compounded no doubt by the fog and the nervousness of the men, a pistol was accidentally fired. The shot was heard by an advanced patrol of the horse guards who gave the alarm, both to the king's cavalry, stationed at Westonzoyland, and to the infantry.

Initially the rebels had the advantage of surprise, and Monmouth ordered his cavalry to charge the enemy. Onwards they rode through the night and fog, expecting at any minute to make contact. What they found, though, was not the enemy, but an obstacle they knew nothing of, the Bussex rhyne; and on the other side, still unseen, the king's army. Monmouth's cavalry then came under a barrage of musket fire, which scattered them into the night, followed close behind by the foot soldiers led by Monmouth. There followed a vicious exchange of gunfire lasting well over an hour. The rebel army, made up of faithful followers and raw recruits, fought bravely, but were no match for the king's men.

As the day broke it was obvious to Monmouth that that the battle was lost. He mounted his horse and slipped away, leaving behind him a scene of devastation. Over 300 lay dead in the field; many more may have died later from their wounds.

Withy Boiler, Aller Moor

A familiar sight around the West Sedgemoor district is the willow or withy boiler. The outward appearance of the harvested withy can be altered in a number of ways, each producing a distinctive look to the rod. The withy can be left to dry with its bark on, producing a brown rod, or can be steamed for a few hours before use, which gives the bark a dark shiny finish. Close by the boiler, standing in shallow rhynes, you will often find bundles of withies stacked upright. These withies are allowed to shoot again: in doing so the sap in the rod rises, enabling the bark to be stripped off to reveal the white wood underneath.

By far the most popular coloured willow is the 'buff'. This is produced by lowering a cage full of willow bundles, or 'wads', into a vat of boiling water. The water is boiled for at least nine hours, softening the bark, and releasing the tannin and other chemicals that stain the wood the familiar red-brown colour.

The bundles are then removed to the stripping shed, where the bark is removed revealing the buff coloured willow. Once stripped the buffs are stacked against wire fences to dry, before being woven into baskets.

CUTTING WITHIES, WEST SEDGEMOOR

The rich clays and high water table to be found in this central part of the Somerset wetland provide the ideal conditions for growing withies. Based on the ancient craft of coppicing, the willow or withy field produces an annual crop of willow rods for at least twenty-five years without the need to replant.

In the first place the ground is prepared as for a normal crop, sowing in the spring, but instead of seeds, sets or short lengths of willow from a previous year's crop are pushed into the ground at regular intervals across the field. These rods will soon put down roots and start to grow. At the end of a year's growth, they will be cut down to within a few centimetres of the ground. This causes the stumps to form numerous new shoots. Repeated cutting will produce stumps of considerable size, sending out many shoots where there was originally only one. Three years after the initial planting the withy field becomes financially viable.

The willows need careful management throughout the growing season from March to late September. In early March any premature growth, liable to frost damage, is checked by allowing cattle to graze among the willows. In order to ensure a straight rod, essential for basket-making, the beds must be kept free from weeds and pests, such as the aphid.

Harvesting starts in mid-November and continues throughout the winter until the end of February. Much of the cutting is still done by hand with a sharpened hook, although young beds, their stumps being softer, can be harvested by machine. The sight of men doubled over, harvesting a crop by hand in these days of 'high tech' agribusiness, seems an anachronism.

CRICKETBAT WILLOWS, ALLER MOOR

Cricketbat willows were given their name for the obvious reason, the straight trunks providing the ideal timber for cricket bats. Although no longer planted for that purpose any more in Somerset, they are still a familiar sight in the wetland region of the county. Their purpose now is to form windbreaks which they do most effectively. Being deciduous they shed their spear-shaped leaves rapidly during the autumn months. When the first storms arrive their spindly branches provide just enough resistance against the wind. Too much resistance would cause the tree to topple, or even worse to produce vortices or turbulence on the lee side, creating as much damage as if there were no windbreak there at all.

The underside of the willow leaf is an almost silvery green, lighter in colour than the top side. In the late spring or early autumn with a good breeze blowing, the sunlight, which is still low on the horizon, catches these as they twist and turn, causing the trees to shimmer and sparkle against the sky.

West Sedgemoor

The lowland regions of Somerset known as the levels and moors are not a natural phenomenon. They are the result of careful land management by generations of farmers. By draining the marshlands they have created some of the richest pasture in England. This unique system of fields and drainage ditches, or rhynes, encouraged the development of a rich variety of flora and fauna. For many years this environment happily coexisted with the needs of man, but recent developments in farming practice have upset this balance here as well as in other parts of the country. During the latter part of the 1970s and the early 1980s the government, on the advice of conservationists who feared irreparable damage to the environment of the Somerset wetlands, introduced measures to protect the wildlife habitat. Several areas of Sedgemoor were designated as Sites of Special Scientific Interest, or SSSIs as they became known. Once an area of land is labelled an SSSI, the landowner must consult the authorities over any change of use of his land, such as crop type, application of pesticide and such like. The true inhabitants of Sedgemoor are an independent breed, who do not take kindly to interference from outsiders, especially politicians and government officials. There then followed a period of bitter disagreements between the local farming community and the conservationists, much of the conflict stemming from poor communication between the two factions. Matters came to head when effigies of the minister of the environment and prominent conservationists were strung up on a series of gibbets on West Sedgemoor, and burned.

Today, however, the RSPB (Royal Society for the Protection of Birds) has purchased the major part of West Sedgemoor, thus affording protection for the many species of wetland bird. The land is also leased back to farmers, who manage the land in such a way that it does not upset the delicate ecosystem that has evolved over the centuries.

SOUTHLAKE MOOR

Deep in the heart of the Somerset wetlands lies an area of land that has remained largely unchanged in appearance since the time of King Alfred. Southlake Moor comprises a number of fields each bordered by a rhyne or drainage ditch. The moor itself is enclosed by a small lip or wall, creating a shallow basin approximately four square kilometres in area.

During the winter months, south-westerly gales produce a build-up of water in the Bristol Channel, preventing the fresh waters of the River Parrett from flowing out to sea. At high tide the level of water in the river is often a good 2 metres above the surrounding land; it is prevented from spilling over by a reinforced bank of earth, which forms the southern boundary of the moor. In severe conditions this flood water is allowed to spill over into the moor. In the past this served two purposes: one, to relieve the river of the flood waters, thus preventing damage to properties further downstream; two, to cover the pastureland with a coating of rich alluvial silt, providing the lush grasslands that Somerset was famous for. Apart from the human element, wildlife also benefited from this action as it provided perfect wintering for many species of wildfowl. Ten years ago a not uncommon sight would be squadrons of swans and geese flying in perfect formation making their way to the lake. However, in the last few years winters have become drier and the need to flood the moor less frequent. The birds, of course, have made other arrangements.

The weather in Britain, as everyone knows, is notoriously unpredictable. In this case a period of severe storms was closely followed by a month of bitingly cold north-easterly winds. The water level on the moor reached a metre in depth, and as the temperature dropped with the setting sun a faint crackling sound could be heard as the surface of the water began to freeze.

THE MUMP, BURROWBRIDGE

At a point approximately midway between Glastonbury and Taunton stands an isolated outcrop of sandstone known as Burrow Mump, or simply The Mump. Although it stands a mere 24 metres high it can be seen clearly from several kilometres away, rising out of the surounding countryside like an island in the midst of a grass sea. This island illusion is, in fact, not far from the truth, for as little as one hundred years ago the moors around the Mump were liable to serious flooding. Undoubtedly the Mump would have used as a fortified position because of the views it commanded over the moors and, perhaps more importantly, the rivers Parrett and Tone, which meet immediately to the south of the hill.

There is a tenuous connection with King Alfred, who in AD 878 built a fort on the Isle of Athelney a kilometre to the south-west. Asser, the Bishop of Sherborne and Alfred's biographer, described the Athelney fort as being surrounded on all sides by an inpenetrable marsh and only approachable by means of a bridge built between two fortresses. It is now known, though, that the Mump was not the other fort, but it is likely that Alfred used it as a part of a larger defensive system to protect Athelney.

The practice of building shrines on isolated hilltops was common enough, even in pre-Christian times, but the earliest evidence of a chapel built on the Mump dates back to 1480, when the Mump was referred to as 'Myghellborough', or Saint Michael's Hill. The list of Somerset chantries of 1548 mentions a free chapel of St Michael, which served the villages of Lyng and Tutteyate (Burrowbridge).

The chapel was replaced by a church in 1607, but by 1645 it lay in ruins. During this same year 120 stragglers from the Royalist Army, having been recently defeated by General Fairfax, sought refuge in the ruins of a church on Burrow Mump. A short time later they gave themselves up, and were taken prisoner by Parliamentary forces under Colonel Oakey. During an excavation of the site a body of a young man was discovered. It appeared he died of gunshot wounds possibly as a result of this incident, or from the Battle of Sedgemoor, which took place some 8 kilometres to the north, forty years later. In 1793 a number of worthies, including William Pitt the Younger and Admiral Sir Alexander Hood, subscribed to the building of a new church, but for some reason it was never completed. In 1946 the Mump and the incomplete church were presented to the National Trust as a war memorial.

THE RIVER PARRETT AND RIVER TONE

The River Tone rises at Baverton Pond in the Brendon Hills and gently winds across the Somerset countryside, through the towns of Wellington and Taunton. From Taunton the river turns northwards on to the wetlands of Sedgemoor. On Curry moor, which lies below the village of North Curry, the flow of the river is regulated by sluice gates; from here on the waters are tidal. The Tone continues for several more miles until it joins the River Parrett at Burrowbridge. The Parrett starts life a little south of Crewkerne on the Somerset/Dorset border and flows in a northerly direction towards Bridgwater and the Bristol Channel. It too becomes tidal, just below Langport.

At one time Bridgwater was a busy port, and both the Parrett and the Tone provided important commercial links with towns inland. The Tone was first made navigable in 1638, when sea coal was taken by barge from Bridgwater to Taunton. Records show that during the 1880s at least a dozen horse-drawn barges a day made the journey between Bridgwater and Langport. The River Parrett was once referred to as one of the dirtiest rivers in England. The thick, brown soup-like waters rush in and out on every tide, leaving vast deposits of silt along the banks. More recently, though, great efforts have been made to clean the river of man-made pollutants. Some fifty or sixty years ago it was common to see small open flat-bottomed boats or dories, known as Bridgwater flatners, pulled up on to the banks of the Parrett. These were often built by farmers, and were both easy to construct and sufficiently seaworthy to survive the choppy waters of the Bristol Channel.

Every year the spring tides of March herald the start of the elver fishing season along the rivers Parrett and Severn. Years after leaving its birthplace in the Sargasso Sea, the young eel or elver arrives at the mouths of these rivers. The tiny elver, still transparent and measuring a mere 2 or 3 centimetres in length, swims, aided by the tide, upstream to freshwater lakes and ditches inland, to mature. At one time the elver was regarded as a local delicacy, to be enjoyed by both rich and poor alike. Today, however, it is very different. The growth of industrialized fish farming and a vigorous overseas market have created a demand for elvers, for the eel will not breed in capitivity. Many people now believe that illegal fishing practices and greed have led to a dramatic decline in elver catches. Despite a scarcity of elvers, a hefty licence fee and a strict policing of fishing methods, you will still find, on a March evening, the banks of the River Parrett lined with 'elvermen' lifting their scoop nets out of the water, ever hopeful that this year will mark a change in their fortunes.

MUCHELNEY ABBEY

Muchelney was once a large island in the marshlands of central Somerset. Flooding still takes place in the winter months, cutting off areas of higher ground. A Benedictine order of monks was first established here by the Saxon King Ine, in AD 762. It is thought that a party of raiding Danes attacked and destroyed the monastery, but it was rebuilt; and a new religious centre was established in AD 950, dedicated to Saint Peter and Saint Paul. Although Muchelney Abbey was the second oldest Christian community in the county after Glastonbury it never reached the same degree of importance. In 1335 the Bishop of Bath, Ralph of Salopia, paid one of his customary visits to the abbey, and what he found there left a lot to be desired. It seems that, because of its isolated position and the infrequency of visits by Church authorities, the monks had embarked on a lifestyle that was not in strict accordance with their religious order. The bishop discovered that the monks had carved a very comfortable life for themselves. For example, instead of sleeping in spartan dormitories they had had luxurious beds made, and had been spending far too much time hunting in the abbey's estates. But what distressed the bishop more than anything else was that they had been entertaining secular men, women and girls within the confines of the abbey. The bishop ordered a complete stop to these activities, insisting that the monks reformed their way of life and refurbished the abbey buildings, which had been allowed to fall into disrepair. It seems, though, that the monks paid little heed to the bishop's advice and continued in much the same way as before. In 1538 one of King Henry VIII's representatives arrived at Muchelney and declared the monks unfit for religious duties, demanding the surrender of the abbey. This was achieved and the buildings were sold into private ownership. Both the monastic buildings and the church have disappeared, apart from the foundations. The abbot's house remains, though it dates from the sixteenth century, and is in good repair. The house is constructed from a type of limestone known as blue lias, which is found locally, and fine detailing is worked in the golden ham stone from the nearby Ham Hill quarries.

WESTONZOYLAND PUMPING STATION

If you can imagine the Somerset moors and levels to be rather like a basin, the sides are made up of three ranges of hills – the Mendips, the Poldens and the Quantocks – and a shallow rim of higher ground forming a barrier with the sea. Winter rains draining off the surrounding hillsides into the streams and rivers are prevented from finding their way to the sea by this rim of higher ground along the coast and the tidal range in the Bristol Channel. Even today large-scale flooding is a common sight, albeit within a much smaller area than 5,000 years ago, when man first settled here. Very little was done to alleviate the annual flooding until the monks of Glastonbury began constructing drainage channels across the Sedgemoor in 1234. This only partially improved the land, as the flood water still had to drain away to the sea by force of gravity rather than by any artificial means. Minor improvements continued to be made to control the movement of water, for example by raising the height of river banks to produce navigable channels for shipping, until the dissolution of the monasteries. Hereafter all further efforts to reclaim land ceased, and the Sedgemoor reverted to its natural state.

During the eighteenth and nineteenth centuries a population boom created a greater demand for food production. The rich pastureland of the Somerset wetlands could only be exploited if some means of water extraction from the lowest part of the moor could be devised. In 1830 an Act of Parliament formed the first drainage district of Othery, Middlezoy and Westonzoyland, designed to manage the moors around these three villages. During this time the first steam-powered pump was installed at Westonzoyland. This new development was to have far reaching implications for the appearance of the Sedgemoor. A network of drains or rhynes were built by landowners, which were linked together, leading to the pumping station at Westonzoyland – situated on the banks of the River Parrett. The efficiency and reliability of the steam engine enabled pumping to take place continuously during the winter months. In all, 648 hectares of land could be drained by this method.

It was not long before similar stations were built right across the central part of the Sedgemoor. The Westonzoyland pumping station is in a remote location and in the early days would have had to be self-sufficient in both food for the operator and his family, and in workshop facilities for the maintenance of the engine. The last operator was a Clifford Thyer, who took up residence with his wife and children in 1920. Both he and his wife would have played an active part in the running of the station until 1950, when the steam-driven pump was replaced by diesel power, which no longer required a live-in operator.

St Decuman's Church

On a hill overlooking the ancient port of Watchet stands a church dedicated to St Decuman. It is said that he arrived from Wales, drifting across the sea on a raft, and accompanied by a faithful cow, that swam alongside. Upon reaching the shore Decuman made for this hill and established himself as a hermit. His strange behaviour did not go down too well with the local inhabitants, who set upon him while he was at his prayers. The legend states that after being beheaded Saint Decuman calmly picked up what simple possessions he had, including his severed head, and set off, together with the cow, back across the water to Wales.

But St Decuman's church is notable for another reason. It is a tragic place. At Orchard in the parish of St Decuman lived Robert Fitzhurse, one of the murderers of St Thomas à Becket. Another lived at Samford Brett, a nearby village, both of them being caught and punished.

There are many very beautiful churches in Somerset, but not many with such a colourful history. Photographically, though, the visual possibilities of the exterior were limited. On the other hand, a close inspection of the graveyard revealed a wide variety of designs, some quite unusual, such as ship's anchors and chains wrapped around the branches of trees. My eye eventually settled upon this little statue, a poignant memorial to the death of a child.

WATCHET HARBOUR

Safe harbours along the north Somerset coast are few and far between. The vicious currents and unusually high tidal ranges make life hazardous for shipping, even at the best of times. Watchet was an active commercial port in Saxon times and is now the only port open to commercial shipping.

In AD 918 the Danes landed and were finally defeated at Battle Gore, which lies in a valley a few miles to the north of Watchet. More famous, though, is the town's connection with Samuel Coleridge's 'The Rime of the Ancient Mariner'. It was on a walk from the nearby village of Nether Stowey to Lynton in Devon that Coleridge came to Watchet, the basis of the now famous poem fresh in his mind. He turned to Wordsworth who was accompanying him and said: 'Here is where he shall set out on his fateful journey.' The following lines are thought to relate to Watchet harbour:

> The ship was cheered, the harbour cleared,
> Merrily did we drop
> Below the kirk, below the hill,
> Below the lighthouse top.

As I walked around the harbour towards the end of the quay, I began to see in my mind's eye an image of the ship sliding out through the harbour entrance past the crowds clustered around the lighthouse. For the crew the last view of Watchet from the deck of the ship would have been of the lighthouse, becoming smaller and smaller as the ship made for the open sea.

KILVE BEACH

Hardly a beach in the normal sense of the word, the brown waves of the Bristol Channel break here on to the weathered terraces of exposed rock strata. These terraces, or pavements as they are known, are formed of blue lias, a type of limestone. Sandwiched between the blue lias strata are layers of a softer rock, which, when exposed to the elements, are washed away leaving the harder limestone behind. A weakness in the structure of the limestone allows further erosion to take place, splitting the material into regular sized blocks. Careful examination of these blocks will reveal what are known locally as St Keyna's Serpents, or in other words ammonites. These are named after the saint, who on arrival in Somerset is said to have transformed all the snakes in these parts into stone.

During the autumnal spring tides there has been a long tradition among the local population of 'glatt hunting'. The glatt or conger eel thrives in the muddy waters of the Bristol Channel, in normal states of the tide existing under the many boulders that lie just beneath the low water mark. However, during the spring tides vast areas of shoreline become exposed. It is at this time that the glatt hunters arrive, armed with sharpened sticks and accompanied by dogs, mainly fox terriers. The hunt itself involves wading around in ankle deep mud, lifting rocks and prodding clumps of weed. Excitement begins when a glatt is discovered, usually by the frantic scrabbling of the dog; this is then followed by a frenzy of mud-whacking by the hunters in an attempt to kill the unfortunate creature.

During their time in Somerset both Coleridge and Wordsworth paid frequent visits to the beach, and in the 1850s Kilve was a favourite haunt for smugglers. It was common practice for French merchantmen to off-load contraband brandy, which would then be transferred to a nearby chantry onshore. Disaster struck one day when the liquor caught fire and destroyed the building. The ivy-covered remains are still to be seen as one makes one's way from the village of Kilve down to the sea.

The Retort, Kilve

Those who picnicked on Kilve beach in the early 1900s would not have been surprised by rocks that were set alight by the heat of small bonfires. For the rocks here are rich in oil, not in the usual liquid form but locked into a layer of shale. In 1916 preliminary bore holes were sunk and subsequent analysis revealed oil rich shale beds to a depth of 300 metres and covering some 3,240 hectares. This was enough, claimed the scientists, to produce 23 million litres of oil a year, making it one of the most important shale oil finds in the world at that time. An added bonus was the fact that the stratum of shale was sandwiched between layers of blue lias limestone, suitable for the production of cement.

In 1924 the Shalime Company was formed to exploit both of these natural resources. The Great Western Railway considered building a new line from Bridgwater, some 24 kilometres to the east, to service this new industry. In order to extract the oil from the rock it was first subjected to intense heat, causing the shale to change its chemical composition and at the same time giving off vapours which were then condensed into oil, by means of a retort. Full scale production was ready to start, but unfortunately it was never to be, as the hoped-for financial backing never materialized. Maybe the initial costs of processing the shale were too high and there was still the problem of the vast quantities of slag, produced as a result of the extraction, which had to be removed from the site. Brief attempts to revive production took place in the 1940s but were unsuccessful. The post-war period saw the cheap imports of crude oil from the Middle East and finally the production of oil from our own fields in the North Sea.

LILSTOCK

Along the coast between Minehead and Bridgwater, lime burning works were built to exploit the natural resources of the area. There was much demand for calcified lime for top dressing fields where the soil was too acid. The easiest way to transport lime in bulk for any distance in the seventeenth and eighteenth centuries was by sea, the road system in this part of Somerset being totally inadequate for this purpose. Although treacherous for shipping this coastline once bustled with activity, the Somerset seafarers being famed for their seamanship and their knowledge of the waters around the West Country.

There are very few natural harbours to be found along the north Somerset coast, so facilities for the exporting of lime had to be created artificially. One such port was Lilstock, where the remains of stone harbour walls and a building can still be found hidden behind a high bank of pebbles. In its heyday there was an elaborate wooden pier at Lilstock, at the end of which was a summer house for Sir Peregrine Acland, the builder and owner of Lilstock harbour. During a particularly violent storm a freak wave washed the pier away, and all that now remains are the stumps poking through the pebble beach.

Hinkley Point Nuclear Power Station

If you stand on the high ground of, say, the Quantocks and view the coastline below you, sweeping north-east towards Avon, your eye will immediately be arrested by the monolithic buildings of the Hinkley Point nuclear power station, dwarfing as they do the farm buildings and cottages of the surrounding countryside. Like most other nuclear establishments Hinkley is situated on a lonely stretch of coastline. Without the presence of the station the landscape would appear somewhat forlorn and abandoned; the fact that it is here only seems to add to this.

The site comprises basically two stations, Hinkley A and Hinkley B. The A station was one of the first of a series of nuclear power stations to be built across the country. Nuclear power as a whole has had a troubled history, and the Hinkley site is certainly no exception. Until recently the workings of this industry have been shrouded in mystery, adding to the misgivings the general public may have had about them.

There have been no major mishaps here, a few minor ones perhaps, which is surprising since Hinkley A is operating well beyond its designed lifespan. In the late 1980s there was a move to increase the size of the nuclear power generating industry, introducing a new range of pressurized water reactor powered stations, starting with Sizewell B. The decision to expand the industry was greeted with dismay by both conservationists and the public alike. However, despite a lengthy inquiry permission was granted to start the construction programme. The site earmarked for the next development was Hinkley C. Shortly after the completion of the Sizewell B enquiry, new evidence on the safety and the economics of nuclear power was brought to light. Armed with this new information protestors were able to mount a sustained campaign against the proposals. There then ensued the largest public inquiry of its kind to be held anywhere. The weight of evidence against the development was so great that permission to build the third station was refused, calling into question the wisdom of expanding the industry throughout the British Isles.

While this may have been a defeat for nuclear power and the Government, it was seen as a triumph for the democratic process. Whether you consider nuclear power as one of man's greatest achievements or one of his greatest follies, the buildings at Hinkley Point will certainly dominate the landscape for many years to come.

SHRIMP NETS, STOLFORD

Stolford is a small village that lies at the end of a single track road. It is a road that peters out on a shingle beach that stretches from the mouth of the River Parrett to the Hinkley Point nuclear power station. In the 1890s there were at least a dozen 'mudhorse' fishermen operating out of Stolford and many others from locations on both sides of the Bristol Channel. Now there are only two who continue to fish in this manner, both from Stolford. The term 'mudhorse' refers to a sledge or surfboard-like contraption that enables these fishermen to cross the vast areas of mudflats that are exposed at low water in Bridgwater Bay in order to reach their nets. The depth of mud, a fine sticky ooze, can vary from a few centimetres in depth to anything up to a metre and a half in places. It is just possible to walk through this mud unaided, but only at the risk of becoming stuck, the consequences of which could be dire, for here the tides move at a tremendous rate. Attached to the base of the mudhorse is a timber framework on which the fisherman lies, thus spreading his weight over a larger area. His feet are then used to push the sled over the surface of the mud. At low tide the fishermen set off for their nets which are staked out across the bay, secured to stakes that are driven into areas of firmer ground. These rocky outcrops that rise out of the mud are known by their individual names, some of which sound very curious indeed, such as Woog-off, Possy, Black Rock and Stegang. The principal catches are grey mullet, eels, flatfish and shrimps, which are collected from the nets, loaded into baskets that are attached to the framework of the horse and brought back to the shore. The origins of the mudhorse are unknown but judging from the design, a crude but extremely effective one, it is likely that the tradition of using sledges to cross mudflats is an ancient one. What is even more remarkable though, to the observer, is the sight of such an ancient practice taking place directly adjacent to and in full view of a nuclear power station.

GURNEY STREET MANOR

It is quite extraordinary that even today, when it would appear that all has been discovered about our heritage, it is possible to make new discoveries. There are still treasures to be found. Gurney Street Manor is one such place. It took its name from the Gurney family, who built it in 1350. The Gurneys were Somerset barons who owned property throughout the county, including a castle on the edge of the Mendip Hills. Apparently they did not regard this manor house as being particularly important as the standard of workmanship is of a poor quality. The house remained in the family for approximately eighty years, when the last of the family, Jane Gurney, married a Roger Dodisham. The Dodishams were rising in importance in the county and had money to spend, so the house was enlarged and many improvements were made, this time the work being carried out to the highest specifications.

The manor house changed hands a number of times over the next 200 years, and each time small alterations were undertaken. However, after 1640 little more was done to alter the basic appearance of the house. Very little is known of the history of the building since then, apart from minor changes, such as window replacements and roof renovations. Shortly after the Second World War a local property developer bought the house and divided up the buildings into flats, fortunately without drastically altering the internal fabric in any significant way. It was then allowed to run gently downhill, and when the owner died in 1984 Gurney Street Manor was virtually derelict.

It was at this time that the Landmark Trust, the present owner, was able to buy the property. What it inherited was in fact a late medieval manor house with all its features, both interior and exterior, remarkably intact. With extensive research and financial help a comprehensive programme of restoration was undertaken, and eight years later the work nears completion.

BEECH TREES, QUANTOCK HILLS

Unlike the bleak uplands of the Mendip Hills, the Quantocks, although quite exposed in places, are altogether more hospitable. The ridge that runs along the centre is open and thickly carpeted in heather, fern and wortle. This ridge is dissected at regular intervals by densely wooded coombes, mainly of scrub oak and ash.

In the late 1790s both Wordsworth and Coleridge settled in the area, having been inspired by the 'wild simplicity' of the landscape. Coleridge took a house in Nether Stowey, in the foothills of the Quantocks, and Wordsworth in the nearby village of Holford. They were befriended by a local man, Thomas Poole, who brought them into contact with the people of the Quantocks. Lengthy excursions were made over these wooded hills, which resulted in a collaboration taking place between Coleridge and Wordsworth called the 'Lyrical Ballads'. These reflected both the beauty of the countryside and the tragedy of the lives of those who lived there. Coleridge's unfinished work 'Kubla Khan' was written in a remote farmhouse, further west near Porlock.

It was at this time that landowners introduced the beech tree to the Quantocks. Normally the beech tree likes a drier climate and well drained soil However, by planting the trees on raised banks of earth, sometimes reinforced with stone, they flourished. Initially these raised banks were used as windbreaks to protect the drove roads that criss-cross the hills. The young trees would have been cut and laid to form hedges. While this method of hedging was effective as a windbreak and field boundary, it was also labour intensive in its management. The gradual depopulation of the countryside over the years led to shortages of skilled labour, especially of those people with a knowledge of traditional rural crafts. These carefully managed beech hedges then took on a life of their own, developing into the fully grown trees we see today.

SEVEN SISTERS, COTHELSTONE HILL

Cothelstone Hill and Cothelstone Beacon form part of a chain of rounded peaks stretching the length of the Quantock Hills. During Elizabethan times each of these peaks housed a beacon fire as part of a countrywide early-warning system, at the time of the impending Spanish invasion. From the top of the hill the coastline of South Wales can be clearly seen, and in the right conditions this clump of beech trees, known as the Seven Sisters, can be seen from the Welsh coast. A little below the summit of Cothelstone Hill lies a manor house, the one-time seat of the Stawell family. The Stawells established themselves here during the fourteenth century. During the Civil War Sir John Stawell, a fierce Royalist supporter, was defeated in a skirmish on the lower slopes of the Quantocks, by General Blake, a Bridgwater man. As a punishment, the manor at Cothelstone was partially destroyed and the surrounding wooded parkland hacked down. Sir John was imprisoned in Newgate, never to return to his estate. After his death he is supposed to have left fourteen sons and seven daughters. Some twenty years later the manor house was once again a scene of tragedy. Another John Stawell, also a Royalist, fell foul of the dreaded assize. Sir John, a fair minded man abhorred the inhumanity of Judge Jeffreys towards Monmouth's supporters and protested at their treatment. As a result, Jeffreys hanged two Taunton men from the outer gateposts of Cothelstone Manor. In 1770 a folly tower was built on the site of the beacon by a Lady Hillsborough, a member of the Stawell family. This was to crumble away through neglect and there are no signs now of its existence. The Seven Sisters too were most probably part of the grand landscaping tradition so favoured by the landed aristocracy of the eighteenth and nineteenth centuries. In 1973 Cothestone Hill and 90 hectares of land were bought by Somerset County Council, to be used for recreational purposes.

FYNE COURT

Fyne Court was the home and workplace of one of England's more unusual scientists. Andrew Crosse was born in 1784 and died in the same room seventy-one years later. He lived the life of an intellectual hermit and devoted his life to the study of electricity. The trees around the house were laced with strands of copper wire that led back to his laboratory. As well as attempting to harness the power of electrical storms he also produced high voltage charges with the aid of an instrument known as the Van De Graaf generator. His experiments were usually conducted at night and often resulted in loud claps and bright flashes of light. He soon became known locally as the 'thunder and lightning man'.

It was in 1837, however, that he startled the world by the announcement that during the course of one of his experiments, insect life had appeared without any apparent cause. He had been attempting to produce crystals of silica by passing an electrical current through a porous stone which had been saturated with a certain chemical solution. No crystals were forthcoming, but after a fortnight he observed tiny white objects projecting from the surface of the stone. Four days later these white objects had thrown out hair-like filaments. Closer inspection of these hairy particles revealed insect-like creatures, which after a further ten days moved their 'legs' and moved away from the stone. Thinking that his experiment had, by chance, become contaminated, Crosse repeated it. This time, however, he ensured that his chemicals were sterile. To his astonishment the same type of creatures appeared, but this time they multiplied in number and continued to survive for several weeks before finally being destroyed by frost.

The story that Crosse had produced life from where there was none brought a storm of abuse from many who regarded his experiments as a crime against nature. Andrew Crosse never claimed he had created life, nor could he offer an explanation for this phenomenon. It is thought that this strange tale attracted the attention of Mary Shelley, who, after attending one of his lectures, formulated the idea for the story of Frankenstein.

Shortly after the death of Mr Crosse large parts of the building were destroyed by fire. What is left has been carefully restored and provides a centre for the Somerset Trust for Nature Conservation; very appropriate, as Andrew Crosse was a great observer of nature and a practical conservationist too.

AGAPEMONE

Next to the Lamb Inn in the village of Spaxton lie the remains of what was once a thriving community of religious visionaries, founded by an unfrocked clergyman named H.J. Prince in 1846. During that summer the uneventful lives of Spaxton's inhabitants were to be changed for ever. Into their midst arrived a succession of well-to-do townspeople and in their wake a party of masons, bricklayers, carpenters and labourers. There followed months of frantic activity, and when at last the dust had settled there stood a fine eighteen-bedroomed house, with servants' quarters, stables, cottages, a church, and gardens all set in an acre of land surrounded by a high stone wall.

The leader of this strange order, known as Agapemone (The Abode of Love), was referred to as The Beloved and was regarded by his followers as the second Messiah. The Lord Prince, as he called himself, would often ride out from the commune, surrounded by his followers (who were mainly young, wealthy, good looking and female), and make for Bridgwater. They were welcomed in the town for, religious lunatics or not, they had money to spend.

For the next ten years or so the Agapemone existed peaceably in the village. But in the spring of 1856 an event took place that shocked the local community and indeed the religious establishment as a whole. Mr Prince, considering himself the embodiment of the Holy Ghost, decided that a ceremony involving the sexual union of a young virgin and himself was an essential part of the religious order of the Agapemone. This ceremony, called the great manifestation, was duly performed in full view of an assembled congregation of saints, as his followers were known.

The news of the ceremony spread like wildfire throughout the country, confirming the opinions of the many critics who believed that the Abode of Love was indeed a cover for a brothel. There were of course outlandish stories, gloriously elaborated, of orgies and sacrifices, but all of these were totally without foundation. For the landlord of the Lamb Inn this was splendid news, as business thrived like never before. Undaunted by these scandals Prince continued in charge of his commune until the late 1890s when, suffering from senility, he was forced to hand over to a younger man. This was the Revd John Smythe Pigott, who was equally enthusiastic in his duties at the Agapemone.

For all the scandal and furore surrounding the activities of this commune, the people of Spaxton all speak well of the Agapemone, for neither Prince nor Smythe-Pigott did anything but good for the community.

WEST BAGBOROUGH HILL

Referred to as either Diana the Huntress, the naked man, or Apollo and his dog, this sculpture clings tenaciously to the side of West Bagborough hillside, screened from the road by a row of mature beech trees that cover the north-western part of the Quantocks. It seems that there were at one time at least ten classical sculptures dotted around the grounds of Tirhill estate. They were placed there in the mid-1700s by Thomas Slocumbe who owned the estate. Little is known of either Slocumbe or the house at Tirhill, apart from the fact that it commanded fine views across the vale of Taunton to the Blackdown Hills in the south and the Brendon Hills to the west. It was said that from Tirhill House you could see, with the aid of a telescope, over 140 churches across the county. In 1850 Tirhill was bought and absorbed into the Cothelstone estate. The house, together with nine of the sculptures, was destroyed and sold as scrap materials. It is evident that the remaining sculpture suffered several attempts at removal before being abandoned, for much of it is either damaged or missing.

THE CASTLE, TAUNTON

The original castle here was built by the Saxon King Ine, in AD 720. He was a God-fearing man who was noted for the fair and just treatment of his subjects and foes alike. The building we see today dates from the reign of Henry I, its use being part military and part ecclesiastical at that time. In 1497 it played host to the imposter Perkin Warbeck, who claimed to be Richard Duke of York, the second son of Edward IV. Perhaps its greatest moment in history took place during the Civil War in 1645, when under the command of Robert Blake the castle successfully held out against a siege by 10,000 Royalist troops. At one point, when both food and ammunition had run out, Blake declared: 'We shall eat our boots before we surrender.'

But one of the blackest periods of English history was to follow a mere forty years later in 1685. On 18 June the Duke of Monmouth rode into Taunton and was greeted as a hero. He was proclaimed later the same day in the town's market-place to be the true king of England, and the town and the castle were bedecked in flags. But three weeks later the mood had changed. The ferocious Colonel Kirke, fresh from his victory at Sedgemoor, drove the remains of Monmouth's army into town. Here he carried out numerous public hangings and floggings. He remained in Taunton for a further thirteen weeks until the arrival of the infamous Judge Jeffreys. Jeffreys' brief was essentially to mete out the vengeance of James II after the battle of Sedgemoor. Using the great hall of the castle as his court, he turned Taunton and the surrounding countryside into the 'killing fields' of England. At least 200 prisoners were hanged, drawn and quartered, and over 800 were sold into slavery, to be shipped out to the West Indies; while women and children were flogged in public. No one was safe from the barbarous nature of the monstrous Jeffreys.

Life is a little quieter now for the inhabitants of Taunton, while the castle has become the headquarters of the Somerset Archaeological Society and the county museum.

DELLER'S CAFÉ: THE OLD CO-OP BUILDING

Taunton lies at the centre of rich farming country, and has always been essentially a market town serving the surrounding area. Like many other west country towns its wealth was founded on the woollen industry. The opening of a canal system linking Taunton with Bridgwater brought a further industrial expansion in the town. By the late nineteenth century both road and rail links again improved Taunton's prospects. In the early twentieth century new developments in industrial practice were taking place. Soon mass-produced cars became available for the first time to a wide spectrum of society. This, coupled with the rise of a wealthier middle class, gave rise to a rapid change in social behaviour. By 1925 over 100,000 cars a year were being made in England. This increase in wealth, mobility and leisure time was seized upon by a firm in Exeter, who set up a chain of specialized restaurants across the west country. The first Deller's restaurant opened in the centre of Exeter and proved to be so successful that new branches soon opened in a number of Devon towns. These restaurants were marketed under the collective title of Dellerland. Rather like chainstores, Dellerland had an easily recognizable corporate identity. The Dellerland advertising campaign extolled the virtues of fully 'electrified' kitchens, where food was prepared and dishes were washed under the strictest hygiene controls that technology could provide. In each restaurant there were facilities for banqueting, dancing and entertaining, all in the best possible taste. Dellerland published booklets for their customers, giving details of road links between each of their restaurants and all the major cities of England. They also included vital information for the discerning housewife on such matters as the correct way to fold a serviette, or where and when one should buy ptarmigan, quails' eggs, royal sturgeon and other delicacies. The last of the chain of Deller's opened in Taunton in 1925, in a converted woollen mill. While the brave new world of high technology filled the interior of this particular branch of Deller's, the exterior seems to have been rather less resolved. The front entrance attempts to be modern, perhaps influenced by the Art Deco movement, whereas the side elevations present a curious mixture of archways and simulated Tudor timber work. Dellerland survived as an institution until the late 1950s, when it was taken over by Cadena Cafés of Bristol. Since then this building has seen a number of uses, either as warehousing or shops. Part of the attraction of this building is its strangeness. Not a particularly elegant structure, it is nonetheless a reminder of a bygone age.

TARR STEPS

Before the days of mechanized lifting equipment many would have believed that this curious structure was the work of the devil. To lift such large slabs of stone would surely have required supernatural assistance. Local stories tell of animals being torn limb from limb by some mysterious force while attempting to cross over. This devilment was eventually resolved by a local priest who, on reaching the centre of the bridge, confronted the devil who was standing on the opposite river bank. After a brief exchange between the two, the devil is said to have called the priest a black crow, to which the priest replied that nothing could be blacker than the devil. From then on both men and animals have used the bridge in complete safety. The word Tarr is thought to be a corruption of the Celtic word for causeway, but the precise age of the bridge is not known. There have been numerous archaeological finds dating from the Bronze Age found on Exmoor, but nothing that could be directly linked with Tarr Steps. Close by, running either side of the River Barle, are two ancient ridgeway tracks. Some have suggested that the bridge might have provided a link between these two road systems. What appears more likely, though, is that the bridge is medieval. The 'clapper' bridges of Dartmoor, which closely resemble Tarr Steps, were built during this period. The construction of the bridge is unusual inasmuch as no mortar has been used to bond the stones together. The bridge consists of large rectangular slabs of rock, some over 2 metres in length and at least a metre wide, placed over upright blocks, which act as piers. There are seventeen openings between the piers and the overall length of the bridge is more than 50 metres. Historical records show that the bridge has been rebuilt on a number of occasions, the most recent being after the severe winter of 1952. It was during this same winter that the tragedy at Lynmouth, which lies north-west of Tarr Steps on the Somerset/Devon border, occurred – meltwater from the snows on Exmoor sweeping large parts of this little seaside town into the sea. Likewise floodwaters rushing down the River Barle destroyed the central portion of Tarr Steps, slabs of rock from the bridge weighing up to a tonne being found some 50 metres from their original position. In this instance the destruction was caused by lumps of ice and timber piling up against the bridge and blocking the flow of water through the bridge. Today, in order to prevent such a thing happening again, wire booms have been stretched across the river upstream of the bridge to catch any driftwood before it can do any damage to this ancient monument.

THE RIVER BARLE, EXMOOR

The central ridge of hills that runs east to west across Exmoor provides the watershed for many streams and rivers that flow both north to the Bristol Channel and south to the English Channel. The two principal rivers of Exmoor both rise very close together in the Exmoor Forest region, at the western extremity of the moor. These are the River Exe, the best known, and the River Barle. Of the two rivers the Barle is the less precipitous, and winds its way through the valleys of Exmoor at a more leisurely pace than the Exe. It passes through the moorland villages of Simonsbath and Withypool, past the remains of the ancient earthworks of Cow Castle and the site of a nineteenth-century copper mine, which failed to provide the wealth and prosperity for its owners that they had hoped for, and eventually joins the River Exe just south of the regional capital of Dulverton.

This is also the hunting ground for the notorious 'Exmoor Beast', a modern legend that has yet to be proved either true or false. A subject of television documentaries and numerous newspaper reports during the 1980s, the Exmoor Beast (an unusually large black cat) has been sighted on many occasions along the banks of the River Barle. Farmers fearing for the safety of their livestock have spent a considerable amount of time trying to track down this elusive beast. Some reports suggest that this creature, capable of killing young deer and sheep, may be anything up to 2 metres in length. Others suggest that it may be an unusual cross between a feral black cat and a wild cat, producing a new species perfectly suited to surviving in this remote part of Somerset.

LISCOMBE FARM

From Norman times, and possibly earlier, Exmoor was a Royal Forest – not a forest in today's sense, but open parkland reserved primarily for royal hunting purposes. In 1540 the historian John Leland described Exmoor as 'Barren and morisch land where ys store and breeding of young catelle'. For a while the forest provided not only a hunting ground for royalty, but also grazing for cattle and sheep. An entry in the Domesday Book listed upwards of more than 30,000 cattle registered in the district of the Royal Forest of Exmoor. By 1815, however, the Enclosure Acts brought to an end the forest as such. In 1818 an attempt was made to tame this windswept landscape, when a Midlands man, John Knight, bought four fifths of the original forest. He brought with him the most modern farming methods available at the time, and built 16 kilometres of stone walls to act as protection for the 8,000 hectares of land he put under the plough. The land was drained and the field limed in an attempt to raise its level of productivity. Despite many years of intensive activity John Knight's efforts were not altogether successful. To say that he failed outright would not be true, but the climatic conditions and terrain were not suitable for the type of intensive cereal farming that he had envisaged. Over the years Exmoor has reverted to its traditions of upland grazing. The quality of the livestock has been improved by the introduction of new breeds such as the Scottish Blackface sheep, which has largely replaced the indigenous Exmoor Horn. Cattle and sheep still form the backbone of the Exmoor economy and help has been given to the upland farmers by the Ministry of Agriculture through ADAS (Agricultural Development Advisory Service), who ran an experimental farm at Liscombe. The size of these stone posts, at the entrance to Liscombe Farm, would suggest that they were built to hang a gate of substantial proportions, perhaps used to protect the farm at a time when sheep stealing on Exmoor was endemic.

WINSFORD HILL, EXMOOR

Winsford Hill is home of one of the largest herds of Exmoor ponies – an ancient breed that can trace its ancestry back to before the Ice Age. Evidence derived from fossilized remains found throughout Europe, Asia and the United States suggests that these hardy beasts originated in Alaska and gradually made their way across Asia and Europe, finally ending up in the hills of Exmoor. Although they closely resemble the Mongolian horse, they are a specific breed of their own.

There are only approximately 800 ponies certified as pure Exmoor left in the world, and they are regarded as an endangered species. They differ from other horses in the anatomy of their mouths and teeth, which enables them to browse off a variety of foodstuffs other than grass, such as moss, wortle and, during the winter months and when snow covers the normal grazing, the prickly leaves of the gorse bush.

Although they live in a wild state, the herds are owned and managed by individual farmers, who have grazing rights over the moor. Every year in October the foals are checked for pedigree and are marked and entered into a register. While the main concentration of Exmoor ponies is still in Exmoor, they can be found in all parts of the world, including Scotland, Iceland and as far away as California.

In winter, Exmoor has been likened to the bare rolling wastes of the sea, with its long heaving monotony of grey water. I would not go as far as that in my description of it, but grey it certainly was as I set out to walk over Winsford Hill, low cloud and a heavy persistent drizzle obscuring the horizon. The ponies stood out against the horizon, and as I approached seemed totally unconcerned by my arrival, completely at home in this desolate landscape.

HURLSTONE POINT

Gore Point in the west and Hurlstone Point in the east form the two extremities of Porlock Bay, a crescent-shaped shingle beach that extends for four kilometres between the two headlands. The coastline along this part of western Somerset is dominated by what are referred to as hogsback ridges, rounded hills that plunge down on one side into the sea. Some 300 metres above Hurlstone Point is Selworthy Beacon, once the site of one of the most important beacons in the county. From here the first fires would have been lit, warning of the approach of an invasion force. The signal would have been spotted from Dunkery Beacon and then relayed right across southern England. Travelling east from Hurlstone and Selworthy Beacon the coastline subsides, becoming altogether less dramatic. Eventually the shallow cliffs between Minehead and Kilve disappear, leaving a shallow ridge perhaps only a few metres above sea level, until the rocky headland of Brean Down is reached on the Avon/Somerset border. Porlock Bay is a unique feature of the Exmoor National Park, a raised shingle beach behind which lie saltmarshes and ponds. This is a valuable area for a wide variety of wildlife, such as wading birds, which feed on the crustacea that thrive in the brackish waters of the marsh. A little further inland is pasture, where supposedly the best malting barley in the country is grown. As I looked down across Porlock Bay towards Hurlstone Point I could see the first of many westerly depressions moving rapidly up the Bristol Channel, soon to engulf the hills above the headland in cloud, thus heralding a week of continuous rain.

DUNKERY BEACON, EXMOOR

At the highest point in the county, some 550 metres above sea level, lies Dunkery Beacon – a desolate, windswept hilltop standing in the most north-westerly part of Somerset. The beacon itself has now gone, and the mound of stones at the summit, placed there in 1937 to protect the hilltop from the ravages of visitors, marks the site of a Bronze Age burial cairn. Although there seems to be an association between the barrows of the Bronze Age and the beacons of later times, it is not quite certain how early in history beacons were used as a means of communication. During the sixteenth century, however, a comprehensive system of beacons was constructed right across the south of England to warn of any invasion. At Dunkery the beacon comprised three large stone fire hearths, 2 metres across, arranged in the shape of an equilateral triangle. At the time of the Spanish Armada a universal method of signalling was devised: one fire provided an initial warning, two fires indicated that an invasion was imminent, and three signified that the enemy had landed. In the event the Spanish fleet sailed up the English Channel to the south and the beacons of Somerset were never lit.

Such is the height of this beacon that on a clear day it is possible to see at least eleven counties of England and Wales, from Herefordshire Beacon in the Malvern Hills to the north-east, to Brown Willy in Cornwall to the south-west – a distance of 240 kilometres. Between 1918 and 1934 a total of 4,050 hectares of land including the Dunkery Hill and the beacon were leased to the National Trust, forming one of the largest properties in the possession of the Trust.

OAK TREES, BRENDON HILLS

Sandwiched between the Exmoor National Park and the Quantocks, the Brendon Hills are an often overlooked part of Somerset. The fertile soils of red loam provide rich farming country and an altogether gentler prospect than the bleak heath-covered uplands of Exmoor. In the heart of the Brendon Hills stands Nettlecombe Court, first mentioned in the Domesday Book of 1086. Nettlecombe is of particular historic interest as it has never been sold, passing by descent through a succession of families from 1165 to the present day. The estate was and still is noted for a wide variety of trees, especially its oaks, some of which have now reached a considerable size. The house is now a centre for field studies, and recently surveys have been conducted in an attempt to date the woodlands that stretch across the estate. Because of local variations in soil types, Nettlecombe displays a rich diversity of flora and fauna. The woodland habitats here have both alkaline and acidic conditions, subsequently studies have revealed an unusually wide range of mollusc species (slugs and snails), together with many types of lichen. The trees shown here were probably part of a larger eighteenth-century plantation. On this particular day the air was crisp and the sky clear, the hillside was covered with a thick carpet of buttercups, and the distinctive shape of the English oak stood out against the skyline.

BURROW HILL FARM ENGINE HOUSE

It is quite possible that iron ore was mined in the Brendon Hills by the Romans. But it was not until the early 1830s that any serious attempt was made to extract this ore in any reasonable quantity. The first commercial extraction took place from 1830 to 1839, when many thousands of tonnes of iron-bearing sandstone conglomerate were quarried in the foothills of the Brendons and shipped to South Wales for smelting. In 1851 a particularly good specimen of Brendon Hills iron ore was displayed at the Great Exhibition, and caught the attention of the Ebbw Vale Company of South Wales. Such was the quality of this specimen that the company immediately acquired substantial mining rights to the region. In 1853 the Brendon Hills Iron Company was formed, and it began to extract iron ore over a wide area of the Brendon Hills. Mining operations started at Burrow Hill in 1860 and the engine house was completed in 1868, built to a traditional Cornish design. It was used for both pumping the mine dry and bringing the ore to the surface. In order to transport the ore to the nearest port of Watchet, on the north Somerset coast, a railway was built. But first a system had to be devised to overcome the difficulty caused by a 300-metre difference in height between the mine exit and the sea. This difficulty was resolved by the use of an incline, which utilized the force of the fully-laden trucks on their downward journey to the sea to pull the empty wagons back to the summit.

By 1877 mining activity had reached its peak. Over fifty mines were in operation, producing a total of over 46,000 tonnes of ore. Unfortunately success was short-lived, for within a few years the country was in the grip of an economic recession. This alone made life difficult for the mine operators, but their problems were exacerbated by the import of cheaper ores from Spain, resulting in the Brendon Hills Iron Company finally going out of business in 1883.

PORLOCK WEIR BEACH

The tiny harbour of Porlock Weir is merely an indentation in the great curve of grey stones that make up Porlock Bay, which stretches from Gore Point in the west to Hurlstone Point in the east. The harbour is essentially a lagoon formed by the sea piling the pebbles into an outer ridge; this lagoon is then fed by a small stream that runs off the steep-sided hills of Exmoor. There is evidence to suggest that a harbour existed here as early as 886, but it was not until the mid-seventeenth century that any significant trade took place. In the early part of the nineteenth century this naturally formed creek was transformed into a proper harbour by the addition of a stone quay and lock gates, which enabled ships with draughts of up to 4 metres to dock at high water. The entrance to the harbour runs due north and is protected from the prevailing westerly winds by a high bank of large pebbles. This bank is not a permanent fixture, as the force of the sea could easily shift this bank and close off the harbour entrance. To prevent this from happening, lines of stout poles have been driven into the beach from the top of the pebble bank down to the water's edge. The constant pounding of the surf and the abrasive action of the stones gradually wear away these stakes until they look like the sun-bleached bones of some gigantic sea creature that has been stranded on the shoreline.

CULBONE CHURCH

Battling through the swarms of biting flies one evening, I followed the winding path through the Tangled Wood to find this tiny church nestling in a clearing at the bottom of a coombe. Culbone church is reckoned to be the smallest church still in regular use in England. Earliest parts of the building date back to the twelfth century. The word Culbone is a derivation of the Celtic *Kil Beun*, meaning the church of St Beuno – who was a sixth-century saint second only in importance to St David. Up until the later 1600s the district was known as Kitnor, and was long associated with human tragedies. Its inaccessibility on the craggy shores of the Somerset coastline west of Porlock made it the perfect location for the banishment of society's unfortunates. Over a period of four hundred years from 1300, Kitnor has supported a succession of religious misfits, a leper colony and, during the eighteenth century, slaves taken prisoner by the British in the East Indies. In each case these miserable groups were left to fend for themselves. In 1280 the assize rolls record that Thomas the chaplain of Culbone church, following an argument with one of his parishioners, an Albert of Eshe, struck out at him and embedded an axe in his head, killing him. Today Culbone is a place of quiet contemplation, its tragic past laid to rest, and despite its remote position receives a steady stream of visitors. There is even a small Christian community here that provides simple refreshments, payment on trust, for foot-weary travellers who make their way along the coast path that runs alongside the church.

PACKHORSE BRIDGE, HORNER

Typical of the many packhorse bridges to be found on Exmoor, this one was hidden among the trees which dip their branches into the River Horner. The word 'Horner' is derived from the Saxon *hwrner*, meaning the snorer, a reference to the sound the river makes as it tumbles over the stony river bed, down the Exmoor hillsides to the sea. The village of Horner comprises a handful of cottages that nestle at the entrance to one of the most beautiful valleys of Exmoor. Woods follow the little stream half-way up the steep-sided hills until open country is reached, where the ground is covered with a carpet of heather and wortle. The river flows through the centre of Somerset's staghunting country and it is not unusual for the prey to make its escape by following the river down to Porlock Bay, from whence it swims out to sea, leaving the huntsmen and their hounds stranded on the shingle beach. The packhorse bridge, constructed sufficiently high above the winter floodwater to avoid a build-up of debris that is washed down the hills, has always been an essential part of the communication system. So important were these bridges that at one time a tax was levied by central government to provide funds for their maintenance, ensuring that they would remain open at all times. In this remote part of Somerset the horse once provided the only means of transport. Nowadays tractors and four-wheel-drive vehicles have largely taken their place, but despite this, these bridges still echo to the clattering of horses' hooves.

BURROW HILL AND TREE

Driving south from Muchelney across the wetlands towards Kingsbury Episcopi, Burrow Hill can be clearly seen with its crown of a single oak tree on the summit. One could easily be mistaken in believing that the hill was manmade due to the symmetry of its shape. There is no evidence, however, to support this notion. Possibly the hill was used as a religious site for pagan ritual, but more likely the tree would have been planted during the eighteenth century, when there was a fashion for landscaping the countryside on a grand scale. A single tree or isolated clumps of trees were often planted in prominent positions, not for practical reasons, but to improve the aesthetics of the countryside. Certainly the practice still continues today, for after the recent storm of 1987 many trees were uprooted, especially those on exposed hilltops. They have all now been replaced.

The surrounding wetlands are still liable to flood, but the lower slopes of the hill provide ideal conditions for cider apple growing, for the apple tree prefers a drier soil. The apples from these orchards are said to produce some of the best farmhouse ciders to be had in Somerset, and probably in England.

CIDER ORCHARDS

While cider making is not confined to Somerset alone, the cider orchard is thought of as being very much part of the Somerset landscape. Until recently the business of making cider has been divided into two camps – farmhouse cider or scrumpy, which is produced in small quantities for local consumption, and the more commonly known carbonated variety, which is mass produced and sold nationally. Large-scale production of cider, however, cannot rely solely on supplies of English apples from local orchards for its raw materials, and instead has to import apples from overseas. This mass production and popularization of an essentially regional beverage may ensure uniformity of quality and flavour, but does not satisfy the needs of a discerning cider drinker. Scrumpy on the other hand varies wildly in quality, some quite palatable, while some might be more suitable as a paint stripper. Julian Temperley of Burrow Hill Farm has set out to redress this imbalance. His investment in replanting and carefully nurturing his orchards back to prime condition, including the reintroduction of some old varieties of cider apple, has paid off in the form of many national awards. More recently he has introduced the process of distilling cider to produce apple brandy. In France the drink produced in this manner is more commonly known as Calvados. Attempts were made by Temperley to use the same name, but the French authorities were loath to allow any foreign producer the right to use the Calvados label, despite the fact that the sample sent to the regional appellation controle met with their approval.

HAMDON OR HAM HILL

Centuries of quarrying have destroyed most of the archaeological remains here, but the ramparts bear witness to an Iron Age fortress of some substance. During the first century BC the hill provided the northernmost 'capital' of the Durotrige tribe. These were followed by the Romans, who established one of their largest forts in Britain here. Its prime purpose was to protect the south-western section of the Fosse Way, which ran along the base of the hill.

It was the Romans who first recognized the worth of the golden coloured 'ham' stone found here, which is particularly good for fine carving and has been used extensively throughout the south-west, for such buildings as Exeter Cathedral, Montacute House, Muchelney Abbey and many others. During the Middle Ages quarrying activities on the hill increased and at one time twenty-four separate quarries were in operation. By 1800 over two hundred people were employed on the hill extracting stone.

The end of the fourth century saw Ham Hill change from primarily a military role to one of agriculture and leisure. One of the county's first fairs took place here in 1100, but these did not last long, despite attempts to re-establish them over the centuries. Ham Hill rises steeply from the surrounding valley, and is best viewed from at least a mile away where one can appreciate its position in relation to the settlement below – although this makes for a poor photograph. Moving closer destroys the sense of scale, so the final solution is to explore the camp itself. A series of shots were taken just as the sun was setting, and the last frame on the roll provided the image I was looking for.

MARTOCK

The origins of this quiet Somerset town are uncertain, but it has been suggested that the word Martock stemmed from two words, Mart and Oak, referring to a weekly market held beside an oak tree. Certainly both the oak and the market did exist here, and the oak tree has now been replaced by a stone pillar, a copy of the Trajan column. The town itself probably grew out of the market, as the woollen industry expanded and weavers and cloth dyers established themselves here. During the early part of the nineteenth century Martock became a centre for the manufacture of kid gloves, although cheap imports from France forced this business into decline. This was followed by tent- and marquee-making, which still thrives today. The architecture of the town is well proportioned, sometimes quite grand, but never ostentatious, containing as it does many fine examples of medieval building. One of the finest parish churches is to be found in Martock, parts of it dating back to the thirteenth century. It miraculously escaped Cromwell's wrath in 1645, when he is supposed to have visited together with General Fairfax. Today the town seems to have survived the onslaught of plastic shop signs that plague so many of our more picturesque rural towns, without becoming fossilized as some sort of living museum. Beside the Trajan column, at the centre of the town, is the eighteenth-century market house, which like so many of the other buildings of Martock is made from the golden ham stone from the nearby quarry at Ham Hill. In this instance the richness in colour of this stone was emphasized by the late afternoon sunlight glancing off the sides of the buildings.

MONTACUTE HOUSE

Considered by many to be one of the most beautiful stately homes of Britain, Montacute combines seamlessly the architectural traditions of both Gothic and Renaissance styles. Sir Edward Phelips, a very successful lawyer, commissioned William Arnold, a local builder, to create a house that would befit his status as a man of increasing political importance. It was Sir Edward who led the prosecution against Guy Fawkes after the plot in 1605.

Building began during the 1590s, at a time when the skills generally used for cathedral building were being applied for the first time to country houses. The house is constructed totally from the golden and easily worked Ham stone, quarried a few kilometres away at Stoke sub Hamdon. This was the perfect material for Arnold to demonstrate his considerable talents for carving and architectural detailing. The house was completed in 1601 and continued in the family's ownership until 1911. No other member of the family ever equalled the first Edward's eminence, most being content to live the lives of country gentry. In 1780 another Edward Phelips commissioned a new façade to be built on to the west front of the house. This was done with great skill, incorporating more fine stone carving which matched the earlier work perfectly, despite being taken from the house of Clifton Maybank near Yeovil.

The agricultural depression of the late nineteenth century forced the Phelips to sell most of their land and the contents of the house, eventually parting with Montacute in 1911. In 1915 it became the home of Lord Curzon who, although only a tenant, contributed to the upkeep and the refurbishment of the house. Montacute was finally put up for sale in 1929, but when no buyer could be found it was advertised for scrap, being valued at £5,882. It narrowly escaped complete destruction when Ernest Cook, the grandson of Thomas, who had travelled to Somerset with the intention of buying a nearby country house, chanced upon Montacute and bought it instead. It was through his generosity that the Society for the Preservation of Ancient Buildings was able to present Montacute House to the National Trust in 1931.

THE BARN, STOKE SUB HAMDON PRIORY

The medieval barn shown forms part of a group of buildings known collectively as the priory. Founded by the Barons Beauchamp of Hatch in 1304, the priory housed and supported a provost and brethren, whose responsibilities included offering mass for the welfare of the souls of the founder, his immediate family, friends and the king, Edward I.

The priory was not exactly a monastery, but its inhabitants were expected to live a quasi-monastic life according to the Rule of St Augustine. It also owned farmland as part of its endowment. The barn, built from the local Ham stone, was used for storing and threshing crops grown on the farm, and may also have been used for the collection of tithes. A variety of crops were stored here including peas, beans, grains and possibly hay, stored inside rather than using ricks.

The last of the Barons of Beauchamp died without an heir in 1361, but the priory survived as a religious establishment. It was not affected either by Henry VIII's dissolution of the monasteries, but it was his son Edward VI who finally put an end to these last remnants of medieval piety. From 1548 the farmland and buildings, now the property of the Crown, were leased to a number of tenants, including a Robert Stone, whose descendants continued to manage the farm until 1650. It was the largest farm in the district and remained as such until 1897, when the land was divided up and sold. The priory and its collection of farm buildings became the property of the National Trust in 1946.

WELLINGTON MONUMENT

The Duke of Wellington was born Arthur Wellesley in Dublin in 1769. His family and their forebears had lived in Ireland for over two hundred years. Educated at Eton and later at a military academy in France, his career in the English army was a distinguished one. By the age of thirty-four he was knighted, having successfully led an overseas campaign. In 1808 he fought together with the Portuguese and the Spanish against the French in the Peninsular War, and six years later was made a duke. Why he chose the country town of Wellington is not quite clear, but his family had distant connections with Somerset, although they owned no land there. While acting as an ambassador in Vienna, Wellington received news of Napoleon's escape from Elba, whereupon he returned immediately to England to take command of the British army – and finally leading them to victory over Napoleon at the Battle of Waterloo.

News of this victory soon reached Wellington, where the townspeople gathered together to celebrate their most famous son, now a national hero. It was decided that a monument should be erected on a prominent hilltop overlooking the town. A suitable site was duly found some 270 metres up in the Blackdown Hills and the Devon architect, Thomas Lee, was commissioned to design and build it. In 1817 the foundation stone was laid, amid great celebrations. Work progressed slowly but steadily, and two years later the Duke himself visited the site, only to spend a short time inspecting the works before continuing his journey to Exeter. Wellington was never to see the project completed, for shortly after his visit the building funds dried up and all work ceased. It took another thirty-four years before any further interest could be summoned up to complete the monument. By the end of 1853 it was finished, the cast bronze statue of the Duke being omitted and the top portion of the pillar redesigned and capped to form an obelisk.

It was intended to arrange fifteen cannon from the battlefield of Waterloo around the base of the pillar. They duly arrived at Exeter docks, but the cost of transporting them to Wellington proved to be too high. The cannon have remained in Exeter ever since, to be turned into mooring bollards along the quayside.

By 1912, however, sufficient money was raised for the purchase of four cannon. They were delivered to the monument, but by 1940 had been sold as scrap to help with the war effort. In 1985 one cannon finally reached the hilltop, where it rests today at the base of the pillar.

ROBIN HOOD'S BUTTS

High up on Brown Down in the Blackdown Hills, close to the Somerset/Devon border, is a group of mounds known collectively as Robin Hood's Butts. They are most certainly Bronze Age burial mounds and as far as one can see have no direct connection with Robin Hood himself. It is thought, however, that Little John visited Exeter on one occasion, but there is no mention that he was accompanied by Robin. In archery terminology the butt refers to either the target or the mound of earth that lies behind the target, presumably to stop stray arrows that have missed their mark. Another possible link between these mounds of earth and the famous outlaw lies with the red campion flower, which grows in profusion along the hedgerows in these parts. The local name for this plant is Robin Hood's flower.

Before any serious scientific studies were made of Bronze Age burial chambers, it was commonly believed that they contained treasure. Their isolated position on lonely hilltops and their association with a dark and distant past encouraged a plethora of strange tales, often with a supernatural twist. Robin Hood's Butts are certainly no exception. One such story involves a local man named Bob Sims, who, convinced of the wealth that lay at the heart of the barrows, gathered a party of men together to conduct a thorough excavation of the site. Work started early one morning and by nightfall considerable progress had been made. The party returned the following day, certain that the treasure would soon be theirs, but to their dismay they found that all their work had been undone. The hole that had been made the previous day had been filled in, and the turf had been replaced: they set about their work, and by the end of the day had made up for lost time. Unfortunately what greeted them at first light the next morning was enough to convince the party that the devil was at work, for yet again all evidence of their labours had mysteriously vanished, with not a blade of grass or bush out of place. The party fled, for the area seemed to be possessed by demons, and no amount of treasure was worth the risk. Sims, however, persevered for a while, although he eventually gave up the unequal struggle and abandoned the project an exhausted and disillusioned man. In 1818 the Butts were reopened: the largest barrow was selected and a trench was dug right into the centre of the mound. Here, in a small chamber, there was a small conical heap of flints, but no treasure.

PHOTOGRAPHIC ANALYSIS

I do not hold with any one particular photographic dogma and the only rule applicable is that there are no rules at all. After all, one is attempting to portray a three-dimensional world in two dimensions. Having said that, experience has taught me that it pays to keep things as simple as possible.

My own preoccupation during the course of this project has been with the quality of light and its effects on the landscape. An American lighting cameraman once remarked when filming in England, 'every shot a damn Rembrandt'. He was of course referring to the inherent softness of the English light, caused by the moist atmosphere. It is at best a transient quality, sometimes lasting only a few seconds, the same conditions never to be repeated again. In order to take advantage of these fleeting moments, I like my equipment to be both straightforward and quick to use. Initially I set out to use the largest format camera available to me, an MPP Technical camera, taking 5 in by 4 in negatives. In practice, however, this set-up proved to be far too slow. For the most part I relied on two formats, 35 mm and 120. In the last ten years both lens and film technology have improved dramatically, enabling one to produce quality results from smaller negative sizes.

The majority of exposures were made on an Olympus OM-1n using a variety of lenses, including 24 mm, 28 mm, and 200 mm focal lengths. The remainder were taken with a Rolleiflex 120 format camera fitted with a superb 3.5 Planar lens. The exposures were made on the following films: Kodak T-Max 100, Ilford FP4 and HP5, and, where conditions permitted, Agfapan 25.

Achieving the perfectly exposed negative is always the goal, not always achieved, but to help I always check my exposures with a Weston Master 5 light meter. As for processing, I have adopted a method from another photographer, which involves a negative pre-wash, with the addition of a few drops of wetting agent before the actual development. The developers used were Ilford ID11 at a dilution of 1:1 for Ilford and T-Max films and Agfa Rodinal 1:25 for Agfa films.

I particularly like the effect of filters on black and white film. The Wratten 25a, a deep red, produces dramatic results, but the necessity to increase exposure by three stops outweighs all the advantages. As a compromise, an orange filter provides all the sky effects that I require without too much loss in film speed.

All prints were made on a Durst M605 enlarger fitted with Nikkor enlarging lens, and the papers used were all fibre based, mainly Ilford Multigrade FB and Agfa Record Rapid.

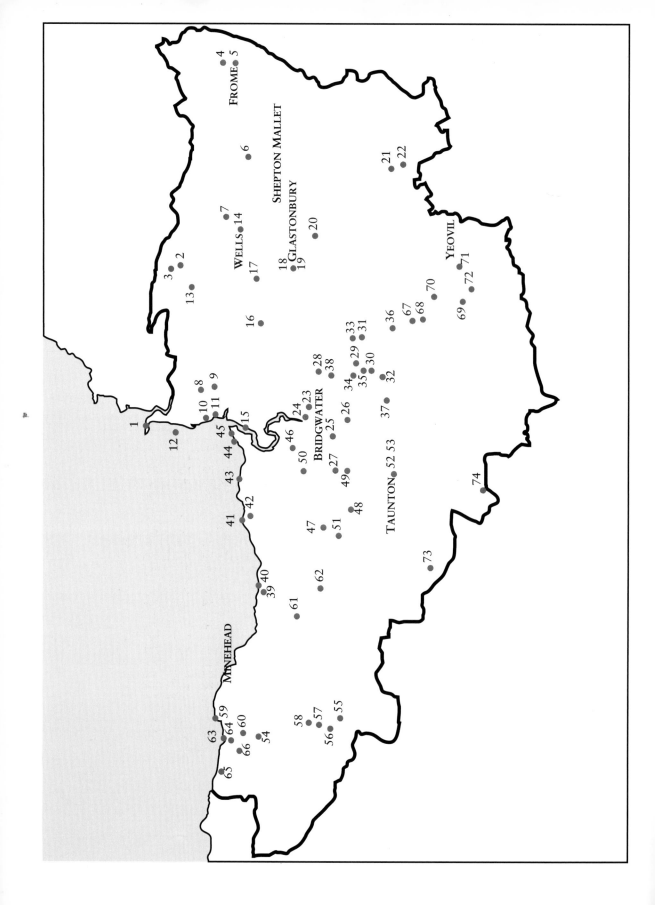

TECHNICAL DATA

key: R   = Rolleiflex
           OM = Olympus OM–1n
           O   = Orange Filter

PAGE NO.	MAP NO.	TITLE	CAMERA	LENS	SPEED	STOP	FILTER
FRONT ENDPAPER	54	THORN TREE, EXMOOR	OM	28MM	1/125	F22	O
TITLE PAGE	22	PARROCK HILL	R	75MM	1/60	F22	
VII	64	PORLOCK HARBOUR	OM	24MM	1/125	F22	
2	1	BREAN DOWN	R	75MM	1/125	F22	
4	2	DRYSTONE WALLS	OM	28MM	1/30	F16	25
6	3	CHARTERHOUSE RAKES	R	75MM	1/15	F22	O
8	4	SUN STREET, FROME	OM	28MM	1/30	F16	
10	5	SELWOOD PRINT WORKS, FROME	OM	28MM	1/60	F16	O
12	6	MOON'S HILL QUARRY	OM	28MM	1/15	F16	O
14	7	EMBOROUGH POOL	OM	28MM	1/15	F16	
16	8	BRENT KNOLL	OM	28MM	1/60	F22	
18	9	EDITHMEAD CHURCH	OM	28MM	1/30	F22	25
20	10	WOODEN LIGHTHOUSE, BURNHAM–ON–SEA	OM	28MM	1/30	F22	25
22	11	SEA WALL, BURNHAM–ON–SEA	OM	28MM	1/60	F22	O
24	12	BRIDGWATER BAY	OM	28MM	1/60	F22	
26	13	CHEDDAR GORGE	OM	28MM	1/30	F11	
28	14	WELLS CATHEDRAL	R	75MM	1/125	F16	
30	15	BRIDGWATER FLATNER	R	75MM	1/60	F22	
32	16	WESTHAY DISUSED PEAT WORKS	OM	24MM	1/15	F16	
34	17	PEAT STACKS	OM	28MM	1/60	F16	
36	18	GLASTONBURY TOR	R	75MM	1/30	F16	O
38	19	GLASTONBURY ABBEY	OM	24MM	1/30	F16	25
40	20	BUTLEIGH COURT	OM	28MM	1/30	F16	O
42	21	CADBURY CASTLE	OM	28MM	1/125	F22	
44	23	BRIDGWATER CLAY PITS	OM	24MM	1/15	F22	25
46	24	KINGS SQUARE TO CASTLE STREET	OM	28MM	1/30	F16	
48	25	CASTLE HOUSE, BRIDGWATER	R	75MM	1/30	F11	
50	26	TAUNTON TO BRIDGWATER CANAL	OM	28MM	1/125	F16	
52	27	THE TEMPLE OF HARMONY	OM	28MM	1/30	F22	O
54	28	BATTLE OF SEDGEMOOR	OM	28MM	1/30	F11	
56	29	WITHY BOILER, ALLER MOOR	OM	24MM	1/30	F16	25
58	30	CUTTING WITHIES	OM	28MM	1/125	F16	25
60	31	CRICKET BAT WILLOWS	OM	28MM	1/60	F16	O
62	32	WEST SEDGEMOOR	OM	28MM	1/15	F16	O
64	33	SOUTHLAKE MOOR	OM	24MM	1/15	F11	
66	34	THE MUMP, BURROWBRIDGE	OM	28MM	1/60	F22	
68	35	RIVERS PARRETT AND TONE	OM	24MM	1/250	F22	
70	36	MUCHELNEY ABBEY	OM	28MM	1/60	F22	O
72	38	WESTONZOYLAND PUMPING STATION	OM	28MM	1/30	F22	O